Teaching the
National Numeracy Strategy
at Key Stage 3

Teaching the
National Numeracy Strategy
at Key Stage 3

A Practical Guide

Pat Perks &
Stephanie Prestage

David Fulton Publishers
London

David Fulton Publishers Ltd
Ormond House, 26–27 Boswell Street, London WC1N 3JZ

www.fultonpublishers.co.uk

First published in Great Britain by David Fulton Publishers 2001

Note: The right of Pat Perks and Stephanie Prestage to be identified as the authors of
this work has been asserted by them in accordance with the Copyright, Designs and
Patents Act 1988.

British Library Cataloguing in Publication Data
A catalogue record for this book is available from the British Library

ISBN 1-85346-738-9

The Geometer's Sketchpad is a registered trademark of Key Press Company.
MSWLogo is a registered trademark of Softronix, Inc.
Omnigraph for Windows is a registered trademark of Software Production Associates
Windows is a registered trademark of Microsoft Corporation.
Microsoft Excel is a registered trademark of Microsoft Corporation.

Printed in Great Britain by Bell and Bain Ltd, Glasgow.

Contents

Preface

The National Numeracy Strategy (NNS) was introduced into primary schools in 1998 (Department for Education and Employment (DfEE) 1998). A Year 7 pilot began in 2000 (DfEE 2000a). Without waiting for the results of this pilot, the DfEE pushed ahead the introduction of the NNS for Key Stage 3, expecting all schools to work with it from September 2001. This was despite the fact that for most secondary schools the final Framework was not available until April 2001 (DfEE 2001).

The project materials may be coming from the NNS, but the framework is a 'Framework for Teaching Mathematics', and as such takes account of the whole of the KS3 mathematics curriculum. Throughout the book we will use 'NNS' to refer to the strategy as a whole and 'Framework' to refer to the KS3 document.

Defining numeracy

You might be wondering about the relationship between mathematics and numeracy, knowing numeracy to be a subset of mathematics dealing with number, and possibly as 'the ability to process, communicate, and interpret numerical information in a variety of contexts' (Askew *et al.* 1997: 4). We prefer the definition offered by a former member of Her Majesty's Inspectorate (HMI) of schools, who sees basic numeracy as the 'sensible use of a 4-function calculator' (Girling 1977: 1), although we realise that such a definition in the current climate is way 'out of order'.

What in fact has happened is that the National Centre for Literacy and Numeracy has been given the care of the whole of the school mathematics curriculum in Key Stages 1–3. They have written the *Framework for Teaching Mathematics: Year 7 to Year 9* (DfEE 2001), building on the previous publication, *Framework for Teaching Mathematics from Reception to Year 6* (DfEE 1998). Their definition of numeracy is all encompassing in mathematics and in other subjects, involving, they say, an understanding of number, measures, spatial problems, graphs and diagrams; in fact the whole of the National Curriculum: 'The definition of numeracy in the *Framework for Teaching Mathematics from Reception to Year 6* is extended here to take account of pupils' growing appreciation of mathematics and the demands of the Key Stage 3 curriculum' (DfEE 2000b: 1/8).

The first definition of numeracy given above from Askew *et al.* (1997) comes from a study by King's College London carried out for the Teacher Training Agency (TTA). In 1997 King's College London started a five-year longitudinal numeracy research study in the primary sector; the Leverhulme Numeracy Research Programme. Some of the data from the Leverhulme study is now in the public domain and we refer to several articles to support our arguments in this book (Brown *et al.* 1998; Brown 1999; Brown *et al.* 2000). It seems that the NNS is using the word numeracy in a way that may have been imported from the USA, meaning mathematical literacy: 'where "mathematical literacy" is a common phase and includes more than number' (Brown *et al.* 1998: 363).

The Framework certainly seems to imply a search for mathematical literacy. It offers an interpretation of the whole of the KS3 programme of study in the National Curriculum (Curriculum 2000, DfEE 1999a). It does give a very positive view of the use of Information and Communications Technology (ICT), although it barely addresses the use of the four-function calculator.

Implementing the NNS

The demand for increase in standards and greater accountability is part of the push towards New Public Management and is found throughout the public sector services including health, police and education. Mahony and Hextall claim that school effectiveness arguments are contextualised in issues of competitiveness, both nationally and globally, and cite the Prime Minister: 'In today's world there is no more valuable asset than knowledge. The more you learn, the more you earn. It's as simple as that. Education is an economic necessity' (Blair 1997, in Mahony and Hextall 2000: 86). Unfortunately it is not as simple as that. Defining knowledge is difficult enough, especially as there will be different interpretations of what is *valuable* knowledge. Helping other people to come to know that knowledge is even more problematic. It cannot be 'fixed' by documents and politicians' pronouncements in the media.

Although the NNS is not a statutory document, we are all aware of the way such national projects become interpreted by external agents such as local education authority inspectors and Office for Standards in Education (OFSTED) inspectors. We have already seen this influence:

> In short, the definition and specification of what it means to be and become an 'effective' teacher became indissolubly tied to the definition of knowledge and knowing as designated within the National Curriculum and as evaluated in 'practice' via OFSTED inspections.
>
> (Mahony and Hextall 2000: 85)

We are sure that this will happen with the NNS and we offer this book, not as propaganda in favour of the NNS, but to make suggestions that may help support the implementation of this new policy. You will need to justify your teaching decisions (especially where they differ from a particular interpretation of the Framework) in response to external pressures. However, Hargreaves points out that mandated change is happening in many countries, with a consequent deterioration and deprofessionalisation of teachers' work: 'Teachers are depicted as being treated almost like recovering alcoholics: needing to adopt step-by-step methods of instruction, or to comply with imposed tests and curricula in order to be effective' (Hargreaves 1994: 14).

Teachers always cooperate with new initiatives, even when they disagree with them. We hope this book will allow you to implement those aspects of the NNS that you value and provide arguments to justify your rejection of the others. New mathematics documents always give a sense of different expectations and interpretations, as do new textbooks and journal articles. We hope this book will allow you to view the Framework as something that can help you and your colleagues to see the NNS as an opportunity for professional development rather than yet another negative criticism of your professional expertise.

Chapter guide

We thought that it would be useful to present an outline of the book, summarising the issues that we have considered. As we approached the NNS Framework we developed various strategies to come to know this particular set of material, its beliefs, philosophies and practices, to decide what was important to address and which aspects of the teaching and learning of mathematics required a re-think. In this section we highlight some strategies presented in the chapters that you may find useful for your own thinking or to use in departmental meetings.

In Chapter 1 we describe the structure of the NNS Framework and introduce the four principles on which it says it is based: expectation, progression, engagement and transformation. Any response to the implementation of the Framework should probably address these issues, and while expectation is high on the political agenda, audits of pupil learning should consider progression and engagement.

In Chapter 2 we offer an introduction to the yearly teaching programmes, the mathematical objectives and key objectives. We do not discuss in detail the images offered by the possible unit plans on pages 1/48–50. Departments could compare these images of the structure of terms within Years 7–9 with their current practice. In attempting to simplify the Framework to a manageable level (there is a lot of detail in the yearly programmes, reminiscent of the first National Curriculum) we use the key objectives and the form of objectives you will find in Section 4 of the Framework. In the chapter appendix we offer tables of the objectives from Section 4, which present the mathematics across the years of KS3, and which may give a useful overview when you are reviewing your current syllabus.

In Chapter 3 we look at the advice on teaching in the Framework and in particular 'direct teaching', the three-part lesson and the consequences of an undifferentiated curriculum. You need to know the definition of direct teaching and the elements of 'good' teaching described in this section. Beliefs in the Framework about expectation are driven by the way it defines an undifferentiated teaching programme for each year (the majority of Year 7 are expected to be taught at Level 5) and in the language and practices of 'catch-up' and 'acceleration'. 'Catch-up' defines failure; acceleration is argued against by most of the mathematics and mathematics education community (UK Mathematics Foundation 2000); many cultures that espouse undifferentiated curricula have a different attitude to measuring attainment. For inclusion within this Framework, we found it useful to look at the demands of the NNS in Years 5–6, and to link the key objectives for these years to those for Year 7 and construct an integrated curriculum that leaves room for consolidation and progression. The three-part lesson is also something that departments need to discuss and in Chapter 3 we offer some examples of different lesson styles. If you are able to discuss the learning benefits of different lesson structures, you are less likely to be encumbered by an external orthodoxy.

In Chapter 4 we compare the language of Ma1 and Thinking Skills. The Framework offers many examples for 'solving problems', which raises the perennial issue of what is meant by 'problem-solving' and 'solving problems' and their relationship to Ma1. The examples from Section 4 (285 pages of them) are useful in lots of ways, although not many are rich in the processes of Ma1. We classified the problems in the 'solving problems' section into three types in order to consider ways of adapting them for working with Ma1. You and your department need to assess the place of Ma1 and Thinking Skills in the implementation of the Framework. Working on the examples as in Chapter 4 offers a way into this discussion.

While based on Curriculum 2000 (DfEE 1999a) there are some differences in the curriculum offered by the NNS. In Chapter 5 we analyse the differences to the content in Ma2–Ma4 as written in the Framework, with particular reference to the changes in geometry. Use the tables in Chapter 5 to work on your own analyses, and to decide how to adapt your current teaching programme. Fortunately, the NNS offers an important reminder to connect the topics and to provide coherent integrated experiences to pupils.

One of the challenges of the Framework is the use of ICT. In Chapter 6 we review the emphasis on ICT in the Framework and categorise the different software identified in the examples. We look at these different categories of software and some of the mathematics involved. We also analyse the solving of a mathematics task using different software and reflect on the results for a learner. Doing mathematics changes with the use of ICT.

In Chapter 7 we consider the role of beginnings and endings in the suggested three-part lesson. All lessons have beginnings and endings and we explore some of the possibilities. No doubt you will be expected at some stage to review how you and your department begin and end lessons and how your current practices fit with the Framework's definitions of oral and mental starter and plenary.

The examples in the Framework offer a way to work on interpreting the expectations of the mathematics in the objectives as well as defining a progression across the Key Stage. In Chapter 8 we use materials from the examples in the Framework to help with planning for teaching for the main part of the lesson. The Section 4 examples offer a wide range of material on which to work and we created a four-stage routine for analysing the level and expectation of the mathematics. One particular set of examples (DfEE 2001: 178–9) gives a set of definitions, which provided a very useful session for discussion with our students. We used the examples given to illustrate these definitions and to think about our understanding of these terms. Overall, the four-stage routine created a system to analyse some of the pages (we had room for three sets of examples) and we have created some activities from these analyses. We took the decision to use ICT where we could, as you can more easily find other types of activities in published texts and the like. You may find the four-stage routine useful with other sets of examples from the Framework.

1 The four principles

The Framework provides a much fuller description of the KS3 mathematics curriculum than is given in Curriculum 2000 (DfEE 1999). It has five sections (numbered independently, so we quote each page number preceded by the section number) and an introduction from the Secretary of State for Education.

Section 1   Introducing the Framework (56 pages) – there are five parts to this section: introduction; teaching mathematics; inclusion and differentiation; assessment and target setting; and planning.

Section 2   Key objectives (5 pages) – these are a selection of objectives from the teaching programmes.

Section 3   Yearly teaching programmes (teaching objectives Years 5–9) (13 pages) – these are grouped under six mathematical topic headings, similar to but not the same as those in the National Curriculum.

Section 4   Supplement of examples, Years 7, 8 and 9 (285 pages) – each double page is divided into four columns, one for the objective and one each for examples for each of the three school years.

Section 5   Vocabulary checklist – this may arrive on a CD as it did in the primary Framework.

The introduction to the Framework states that the NNS was established in 1998 with the target that 75 per cent of 11-year-olds achieve at least Level 4 in the National Curriculum tests by the year 2002. The extension into KS3 is that 75 per cent of 14-year-olds achieve at least Level 5 in mathematics by 2004, rising to 85 per cent by 2007. In order to achieve these aims the Framework is based on the four principles of expectations, progression, engagement and transformation:

- Expectations: establishing high expectations for all pupils and setting challenging targets for them to achieve

- Progression: strengthening the transition from Key Stage 2 to Key Stage 3 and ensuring progression in teaching and learning across Key Stage 3

- Engagement: promoting approaches to teaching and learning that engage and motivate pupils and demand their active participation

- Transformation: strengthening teaching through a programme of professional development and practical support

(DfEE 2001: 1/2)

In this chapter we introduce these principles and explore some of the beliefs and philosophy about teaching and learning behind the NNS and, in particular, the ways in which each of the four principles are built into the Framework.

The principles

Expectations

> establishing high expectations for all pupils and setting challenging targets for them to achieve
>
> (DfEE 2001: 1/2)

Certainly the NNS sets out a great challenge in terms of the defined expectations for all pupils in terms of improved tests results. The National Curriculum, upon which the Framework is based, gives the expected range of levels for pupils working in a Key Stage as well as the expected attainment for the majority of pupils at the end of the Key Stage (Table 1.1). (Earlier documents had this as the level expected for an average pupil at the end of a Key Stage, and not the majority).

Table 1.1 National Curriculum expected attainment during the Key Stages

	KS1	KS2	KS3	KS4	
Range of Levels during the Key Stage	1–3	2–5	3–7	Foundation for pupils below Level 5 at KS3	Higher for pupils at or above Level 5 at KS3
Expected attainment for the majority at the end of the Key Stage	2	4	5/6	National qualifications GCSE	National qualifications GCSE

The National Curriculum defines a programme of study for working mathematically across the Key Stage. As to attainment and the use of the level descriptions for assessment, it suggests, 'The level descriptions provide the basis for making judgements about pupils' performance at the end of key stages 1, 2 and 3' (DfEE 1999: 86). The NNS has taken a different decision. It has not used the Key Stage approach but has defined the expected level of work for the majority of pupils in *each school year* as well as increasing the expectation for children in Year 9 to be working on Level 6.

The Framework then defines yearly teaching programmes for Years 7–9 (Section 3) based on these expected levels of working, which are beyond the expectation of 85 per cent of Year 9 pupils being at Level 5. Thereby hangs the tale. Just because a politician declares that there will be an increase in standards, via an increase in attainment in timed written tests, and just because these increases in attainment become

Table 1.2 NNS expected level of work for school for Years 5–9

Year 5	Revision of Level 3 but mainly Level 4
Year 6	Consolidation of Level 4 and start on Level 5
Year 7	Revision of Level 4 but mainly Level 5
Year 8	Consolidation of Level 5 and start on Level 6
Year 9	Revision of Level 5 but mainly Level 6
Year 9 for able pupils	Objectives at Level 7, with some Level 8

defined in a policy, does not make them happen automatically! As for the teaching programmes, there is an old adage that it is possible to teach any mathematics to anyone at some level. So when devising a teaching sequence for pupils it is possible to work with most content from any Level (see the section on inclusion in Chapter 3). The problem comes with the system being driven and led by tests (solely written tests) with a Framework that includes teaching programmes that expect almost all pupils to move along the same learning path at an identical rate through a school year. Would that it were that easy! Needless to say (and apologies to those who think this an obvious statement) defining a discrete teaching programme like the one in the Framework does not mean that the learning will tidily follow. There is plenty of research evidence to show that the rhythms of teaching and learning are different. Similarly, saying that all 14-year-olds will be above the current average attainment also will not happen because a politician has declared that it should be so.

However, the good news for those implementing the Framework is that its deliberate and overt connection with the National Curriculum – the only statutory and legal document – allows a department to act sensibly, within the bounds of the material in the Key Stage programme of study, rather than the potential straitjacket of the Framework.

Progression

> strengthening the transition from Key Stage 2 to Key Stage 3 and ensuring progression in teaching and learning across Key Stage 3
>
> (DfEE 2001: 1/2)

The same group has written the Framework for the primary and secondary sector, creating a certainty of approach and intention. The advice on teaching builds directly from the expertise of the primary Framework. The KS3 Framework maintains many of the approaches to teaching, such as mental methods and organisational structures like whole-class teaching and the three-part lesson. The stranding and interpretation from the mathematics in the programme of study of the National Curriculum also builds on the work of the KS2 Framework. (In Chapter 2 we consider the presentation of the mathematics in more detail.)

The Framework presents an overview of the National Curriculum attainment targets on which the programme is based (Section 1, pages 9–19). You will find useful connections here:

- Ma2: The approach to calculation: from KS2 to KS3 (pages 10–13).
- Ma3: Introducing and developing algebra (pages 14–15).
- Ma4: Shape, space and measures (pages 16–17), which immediately begins 'Geometry in Key Stage 3 is the study of points, lines and planes and the shapes they can make, together with a study of plane transformations'.
- Ma5: Handling data (pages 18–19).
- Ma1: Using and applying mathematics and thinking skills (pages 20–22).

The Framework slightly changes the organisation of the five National Curriculum attainment targets, using six strands with a recognisable but slightly different form of words and labels (DfEE 2001: 1/45). The following structure is obvious in Sections 3 and 4.

- Using and applying mathematics to solve problems
- Numbers and the number system
- Calculations
- Algebra
- Space, shape and measures
- Handling data

Each of the yearly programmes for Years 7–9 has these strands as headings under which there are bulleted mathematics objectives, a selection of which have been classed as key objectives and given in Section 2. There are units of work for each year, with hours attached. Ma1 seems almost to be an afterthought; it is written in a box running down the side of the diagram rather than being integrated. Finally, Section 4 has objectives accompanied by exemplar questions explaining interpretation of the objectives: 235 pages of them!

Progression and continuity appear to be defined by the Framework, but in reality they cannot be ensured by it. There are still problems about knowing what a pupil knows from a reported Standard Assessment Task (SAT) score; transfer from KS2 to KS3 still needs to be addressed. Concern about performance in league tables grips most schools and therefore there will undoubtedly be a lot of teaching for the test at the end of KS2 (just as there is in all secondary schools for 16+ examinations), with implications for the long-term learning of mathematics. Add to that the fact that the external tests at the end of a Key Stage are marked as percentage scores but are reported as a Level. How does the next teacher know what a pupil knows? The declared Level 5 or Level 4 could mean all sorts of things.

In Chapters 4, 5 and 6 we look at the interpretation of the National Curriculum programmes of study in the Framework, identifying new material and new labelling. In Chapter 8 we look at ways to use the hundreds of examples given in Section 4.

Engagement

> promoting approaches to teaching and learning that engage and motivate pupils and demand their active participation
> (DfEE 2001: 1/2)

Section 1 of the Framework gives advice on teaching, which we explore in depth in Chapter 3. Here we give a brief introduction to some of these ideas.

Raising standards is at the heart of the NNS and its authors looked abroad for practices in other cultures that might be imported to support the aim. Hungarian classrooms, Taiwanese classrooms and Japanese classrooms were visited. There are already many myths flying around about imported practices. Whole-class teaching, direct teaching and the three-part lesson are probably the most talked about, with the undifferentiated curriculum being a fairly new phenomenon. However, as you might imagine, importing the practices and structures from different countries without the rest of the culture has the potential to trivialise the teaching acts that are much more subtle and professional in their initial creation. But the Framework does acknowledge this. For example, of the three-part lesson the Framework says: 'This outline is not a mechanistic recipe to be followed. Use your professional judgement to determine the activities, timing and organisation of the beginning, middle and end of the lesson to suit its objectives' (1/28). So let's raise a cheer for the sensible teacher as acknowledged in the Framework: the critically intelligent professional, who will make decisions based on the needs of the learners and their responses to the lesson, and import practices whose purpose is understood. If this means having a silent lesson then so be it. If this means doing a talk over three lessons, then why not? In Chapter 3 we discuss the possibilities of teaching actions and planning and lesson structures.

Within the policy there are also a significant number of examples that use ICT, spreadsheets, graphing and geometry packages and LOGO, as well as graphical calculators. We devote the whole of Chapter 6 to the use of ICT. If your department does not have much access to computer hardware you will find plenty of support within this policy to request more machines.

The Framework document offers very little discussion of the learner; its main emphases are on content, timing and types of teaching. The Framework is written for most pupils, who are supposed to be average, and is supposed to be sufficient for all. For the bright pupil the Framework suggests following the yearly programme for the year above, accelerating through the curriculum. For the below average pupil they must play catch up, working on the expected curriculum while catching up on what they do not know. One of the aims of the Framework is to 'provide catch-up classes for all Year 7 pupils who did not previously achieve level 4 in English and mathematics' (DfEE 2001: 1/2).

In Chapter 3 we explore these issues further, but attainment of the below average and acceleration of the above average are a major thrust of the Framework and will be of considerable importance to departments.

Transformation

> strengthening teaching through a programme of professional development and practical support
> (DfEE 2001: 1/2)

At the time of writing this book, regional directors and numeracy consultants are being appointed all around the country. The model of professional development is a cascade model with 'experts' supporting implementation in schools. No doubt videos and materials will be given to departments. Some or all of them will be useful, but there is no doubt that the main tool for implementing this policy is you.

One of the by-products of the imposition of a new policy for schools is that colleagues must meet to decide how to respond. It is the process of talking, debating and arguing about meaning and ways to integrate and account for the new policy that will be of benefit to departments; it is the process of talking that might affect beliefs about teaching and learning. Meeting and debating with colleagues from other schools will also be invaluable. This book takes on the role of another advocate. We offer our interpretations about meaning and intention for you as a sounding board for your own ideas. Throughout the book there are situations to debate in your department.

The reality

Unfortunately, although not unexpected from such a politically driven policy, schools that are attaining below the expected national average will be expected to 'adjust' their curriculum in favour of the Framework. This is stated in the section on raising standards, particularly in the first bullet point of the six.

> The factors below should influence the degree to which a mathematics department adjusts its current practices and follows the Framework in detail:
>
> - Pupils' past, current and expected attainment in mathematics and the extent to which the department is likely to meet its target for raising standards
>
> (DfEE 2001: 1/3)

Here are three hypothetical and different stories of schools and mathematics departments that would be found in any inner city area with a mix of socially deprived and wealthy areas. They are types of schools that you will know of and possibly have worked in. Different schools will have to handle their accounting for expectation and progression in very different ways. These example schools have very different catchment areas and attainment of pupils arriving to school in Year 7. What would you advise?

Leafy Green is comprehensive school in a middle-class area, with aggressive competition from surrounding schools, including grammar schools in the vicinity. Parading examination results publicly is a local pastime of the head teachers. The head teacher of Leafy Green has set high targets for improvement and requested that the school use the newly published Qualifications and Curriculum Authority (QCA) Year 7 and Year 8 tests. The school has a high percentage of pupils arriving in Year 7 with SATs results reported at Level 5; most of the rest have a Level 4 score. Surprised by the high level of attainment, by the fact that the teachers' assessment of these pupils' mathematics did not match this assessment and therefore driven by concern for their own audit of potential add-on value, the pupils were tested again with other published tests. The pupils obtained significantly lower scores than the SATs results. The pupils may be able to answer these test questions in May, but they could not repeat this in October. For many their Level 5 attainment was insufficient foundation for further learning. The members of the department are nervous about expectations and have filed these results in case corroboration is needed about the success of their own teaching. The department has imported the whole of the Framework draft Year 7 teaching programme.

Smokey Brown is a school in a socially deprived area, where unemployment and the local crime rate are high. Keeping mathematics teachers in the department is a yearly challenge. Most of the Year 7 pupils arrived in September with SATs scores at Levels 2 and 3, with very few having Level 4. Nearly the whole cohort is below the national expectations. The head of mathematics is very concerned that he will be found wanting by the system. Most of his Year 7 pupils are expected to play 'catch-up' with the Level 4 material, with its suggested aggressive testing regime, while working on the Level 5 yearly programme for Year 7. He knows that this is an impossible task. He also knows that he will be expected to implement the Framework.

Smooth Blue is a school in an area similar to Leafy Green, with most Year 7 pupils arriving with Levels 4 and 5 in their SATs scores. The head teacher has a relaxed view about short-term attainment since the department's General Certificate of Secondary Education (GCSE) results are above the national average and there is a good A-level uptake. The department has not yet decided what to do about the Framework, but since standards in the school are good there is no urgency. The head teacher is allowing the department to make its own decisions.

So, if we take expectation, progression and engagement as defined in the NNS, which of these is the most important? Well, clearly the political answer for all the schools is expectation; the league tables ensure this. Smooth Blue has permission not to act because its GCSE results are good. Smokey Brown has to use the NNS, because its intake has to catch up, but how does the department do this without sacrificing progression and engagement to expectations determined elsewhere? As Leafy Green has discovered, it needed to collect its own evidence to support all its achievements, and to argue its case about added value rather than wait for the results of the public examinations. It may be able to fulfil current expectations, but is worried that any future value-added reporting may see the department being expected to account for progression.

Summary

The Framework has four main sections, and the vocabulary, although useful, is unlikely to be very prominent in decision-making. The first section contains a description of the beliefs of the NNS, its views of teaching and the expectations for teachers and pupils. It is this section that sets out the types of activity that will be expected by those who look at the implementation of the Framework. The three other sections offer us similar material to the many syllabuses and specimen papers we have met over the years (in Chapter 2 we look at this in more detail). The principles of expectations, progression, engagement and transformation set out an excellent value system, but the interpretation of the role of these principles can cause conflict Prescription of teaching styles (which we discuss in Chapter 3) may not lead to transformation and the strengthening of teaching. Conflict between expectations, progression and engagement is an issue of which teachers of mathematics are well aware.

Teachers will have to work on their own transformation, alongside the professional development that is provided by the NNS, if they are to work out ways to implement the Framework. New initiatives offer opportunities for departmental discussion. The major issue will be to find the best balance of expectations, progression and engagement for the learners in your school.

2 The teaching programmes

Teaching is concerned with enhancing pupils' development; it's a *sine qua non*. We would not work as teachers unless we thought that we could help pupils to learn better with our help. The most important question is, what is it to learn better? How do we account for progress in the learning of mathematics? Does the Framework add to our understanding of the National Curriculum and the ways in which society expects our pupils to learn mathematics?

As a teacher I should be able to account for statements such as 'Mary is making good progress', but what does this mean? It might mean that Mary was at point x in the curriculum and is now at point y, or possibly that Mary knew x but now knows it better. The former might describe progress as movement through a teaching sequence and the latter reflects personal progress in mathematics. The former is about teaching, the latter about learning, and thereby lies a dilemma, but a dilemma that is part of being a teacher and that has been in existence for ever. Research (Denvir and Brown 1986a, b; Brown *et al.* 1998) shows that the rhythms of learning and teaching are different and individual. Teaching will affect what is learnt but cannot determine it: 'pupils can learn that which is not taught, while failing to learn what is taught' (Brown 1993: 16). This advice is reiterated in the findings from the Leverhulme study: 'This is in line with other research that suggests that children do not necessarily learn the mathematics that they are taught' (Brown *et al.* 1998: 366). So an important issue for any teacher and any department when planning the curriculum over KS3, is to match the teaching sequence, and the coverage of the curriculum, with the path of development of the pupil.

The Framework

The National Curriculum in its current form has a KS3 syllabus and Level descriptions which it suggests be used for assessment purpose at the end of a Key Stage. The NNS offers a different approach to the presentation of the school mathematics curriculum, presumably in response to the fact that 'the Government intends to set ambitious targets for achievement in the National Curriculum tests for mathematics by 2007, with a milestone target for 2004' (DfEE 2001: 1/2). The Framework provides yearly teaching programmes (Section 3); sets of objectives of what to teach over the course of each year, based on the National Curriculum programmes of study for the Key Stage. The solution offered is one of greater detail and prescription, with many objectives and pages of examples, and suggestions of how much time your learners need. These yearly programmes reflect a route through the curriculum covering the work for each of the years in KS3. It is a teaching sequence, not a learning sequence, but this is nothing new. It is a 'normal' starting point for most departments. Most teachers use schemes of work and use them to account for the coverage of the curriculum. Most teachers have been doing this for ever: reading the scheme/syllabus, looking at what is expected in the examination/test and then planning activities accordingly with or without a text book. GCSE boards offer syllabuses and examination papers. When these change the syllabus is checked and the specimen papers are worked through. The National Curriculum, the legal, statutory basis for the NNS, offers a syllabus ('pupils should be taught to . . .') and level descriptions (the type and range of performance of a pupil working at that level). The Framework is no different and offers a syllabus ('pupils should be taught to . . .') and exemplar questions ('as outcomes pupils should . . .'). The perennial challenge is to transform the teaching aims into learning outcomes.

As we described in Chapter 1, the Framework organises the curriculum into six mathematical strands for each year (DfEE 2001: 1/45).

- Using and applying mathematics to solve problems
- Numbers and the number system
- Calculations
- Algebra
- Space, shape and measures
- Handling data

The presentation of the mathematics under these headings is in the form of detailed bulleted objectives. The objectives are taken from the National Curriculum programme of study but at a level indicated in Table 2.1, presumably referenced against the National Curriculum Level descriptions. Table 2.1 shows the number of bulleted objectives for each year.

Table 2.1 Number of objectives in the yearly programmes

	Year 7 Mainly Level 5	Year 8 Level 5/6	Year 9 Mainly Level 6	Year 9 for able pupils Level 7/8
Number of objectives	62	64	67	42

One logical response might be to divide the objectives over the term: 60 objectives per year, 20 objectives per term, ten objectives each half term, so about two per week, allowing for revision and testing. Silly, isn't it? It's an accountant's response and impossible for most pupils to attain at this rate. In fact the Framework only differs from the syllabuses we are used to by the bulk of detail and the levelling of the teaching programme for each of the years in KS3. It does not offer any real detail on teaching, and certainly it offers none on learning. There is no advice in any of the documents on how to move from the teaching aim to the learning outcome other than by inference. But very little of the content is unfamiliar, other than an emphasis on Euclidian geometry and proofs. The Framework can be managed by linking topics and working on different contexts to practise material that needs revisiting.

Fortunately, the Framework provides some objectives that are more important than others (the key objectives) and using these might provide a way into planning the curriculum.

Key objectives

The considerable detail offered in the yearly programmes in the Framework recalls the very first writing of the National Curriculum, with its 14 attainment targets and hundreds of bulleted, levelled, discrete statements of mathematics. However, unlike the National Curriculum, which over a period of ten years was re-presented in reduced and summarised format, the Framework includes its own summary. Key objectives are given for each year and they are a selection of objectives from the yearly programmes.

Key objectives are given in Section 2 of the Framework folder. These are a selection from the yearly programme objectives to which you are asked to give priority. The NNS explains the purpose of the key objectives:

> Some of the objectives in the yearly teaching programmes are more critical than others. These **key objectives** are highlighted in bold type since they are central to pupils' achievement in relation to the National Curriculum level descriptions. The key objectives should be given priority when you are planning work and assessing pupils' progress. (DfEE 2001: 1/4, original emphasis)

Table 2.2 shows the number of key objectives for Years 7–9. They are given priority because of their relationship to the level descriptions in the National Curriculum.

Table 2.2 Number of key objectives

	Year 7 Level 5	Year 8 Level 5/6	Year 9 Level 6	Year 9 for able pupils Level 7/8
Number of key objectives	14	15	15	13

Table 2.3 shows the key objectives for Year 7. Concentrating on this more manageable list might help to maintain a sense of the mathematics for the year, to develop assessment at the end of the year and also to create an inclusive curriculum for those pupils who have not achieved the national average level in their attainment.

These objectives give a manageable picture of the whole year, while still offering a challenge; if Ma1 is taken as integrated into the whole curriculum there still remain 13 objectives. You will find similar lists for the other two years.

Next it would be useful to maintain connections and a sense of progression across the three years. For this we suggest you look at Section 4 and the exemplar materials.

Exemplar materials and objectives

In Section 4 there are 285 pages of exemplar materials with lots and lots of ideas for the classroom (more of this in Chapter 8). In this section there is also an interesting organisation of the objectives, a summary across the years, which might be useful for thinking about progression in the Key Stage without being overwhelmed by details.

Tables 2.4 and 2.5 show all the algebra for KS3; yes, all the algebra. There is something very comforting about these tables. They show you all you need to know and create a sense of a whole, continuous curriculum. Objectives to the left in Tables 2.4 and 2.5 have examples for all the years of the Key Stage, objectives in the middle are for Year 3 and Year 9 and those to the right are for Year 9 only.

Table 2.3   Year 7 key objectives

Ma2	1	Simplify fractions by cancelling all common factors; identify equivalent fractions
	2	Recognise the equivalence of percentages, fractions and decimals
	3	Extend mental methods of calculation to include decimals, fractions and percentage
	4	Multiply and divide 3 digit by 2 digit whole numbers; extend to multiplying and dividing decimals with one or two places by single digit whole numbers
	5	Break a complex calculation into simpler steps, choosing and using appropriate and efficient operations and methods
	6	Check a result by considering whether it is of the right order of magnitude
	7	Use symbols to represent unknown numbers and variables
	8	Know and use the order of operations and understand that algebraic operations follow the same conventions and order as arithmetic operations
Ma3	9	Plot graphs of simple linear functions
	10	Identify parallel and perpendicular lines; know the sum of the angles at a point, on a straight line and in a triangle
	11	Convert one metric unit to another; read and interpret scales on a range of measuring instruments
Ma4	12	Compare two simple distributions using the range and one of the mode, median or mean
	13	Understand and use the probability scale; find and justify probabilities based on equally likely outcomes in simple contexts
Ma1	14	Solve word problems and investigate a range of contexts, explain and justify methods and conclusions

Table 2.4   Algebra: equations, formulae and identities

Section 4	Year 7	Year 8	Year 9
112	Use letter symbols and distinguish their different roles in algebra		
114	Know BODMAS and use index notation and laws		
116	Simplify or transform algebraic expressions		
122	Construct and solve linear equations, selecting an appropriate method		
126			Solve a pair of simultaneous linear equations
130			Solve linear inequalities in one variable, begin to solve in two variables
132			Use systematics trial and improvement
136		Solve problems involving direct proportion	
138	Use formulae		

Table 2.5   Algebra: sequences, functions and graphs

Section 4	Year 7	Year 8	Year 9
144	Generate and describe sequences		
148	Generate sequences using term-to-term and position-to-term definitions		
154	Find the nth term		
160	Express functions and represent mappings		
164	Generate points and plot graphs of functions		
172	Construct functions arising from real-life situations		

Take, for example, 'Construct and solve linear equations' (DfEE 2001: 4/122). The exemplar material reflects a familiar progression for getting better at solving linear equations and for coming to know more about solving linear equations. You can refer to this when teaching different attainment ranges in the different years. The remainder of the objectives have been collated in a similar way at the end of this chapter for reference.

Units of work

With its planning grids, the Framework gives an outline structure to the teaching year as well as definitions of long-term, medium-term and short-term plans. There are suggestions for units of work for each year showing how to convert the long-term aims into medium-term plans. These units of work cover the mathematics of the yearly teaching programme through a timed teaching programme with hours attached to the units of work. Ma1 is attached to the side of this diagram. Pause before you embark on any reconstruction of your curriculum. The Framework is based on the National Curriculum, and your school will have yearly syllabuses that will match the National Curriculum. In Chapter 5 we report on the new elements of the curriculum. It is only these that you really need to address.

These medium-term plans are most likely to be devised in departments, with the development of a school scheme. You may need to do some auditing of the Framework objectives as you review your scheme. Coverage of the objectives is demanded by the framework.

> Medium-term plans show the titles of units of work or main topics that the pupils will be taught over a half-term or term. Each unit covers a block of several lessons. There are four basic requirements for each year group:
>
> - for each unit, the number of hours or lessons is specified;
> - the objectives to be addressed in each unit are identified, with adjusted objectives for higher and lower attainers;
> - for the majority of pupils in each year – that the units between them cover all the objectives for the year;
> - taken as a whole the units provide breadth and balance across the National Curriculum programmes of study. (DfEE 2001: 1/44)

The learner is not mentioned. As we mention at various points in this book, at some stage you will need to stand up for the learner. The NNS seems to imply that because you teach something the pupils will learn it, which we know is not true. The only time the needs of the learner are addressed in this context is in the statement: 'The best medium-term plans provide opportunities to revisit topics and to make connections between different aspects of mathematics. They also build in time for regular assessment and review' (1/44). Therein lies the tension in the document. There are conflicting messages from the NNS with coverage and delivery of the curriculum on the one hand and making connections and links on the other. The primary Framework (DfEE 1998) offers week-by-week objectives: 'The scheme of work suggested in the Framework maintains the rapid change and recapitulation model, with a tendency to fragment the curriculum into many detailed objectives to be taught separately in logical sequence' (Brown *et al.* 1998: 368). This approach through detailed objectives can lead to the reinforcement of the race through the curriculum and the model of progression as a netting-in as many topics a possible. This is in conflict with the National Curriculum approach to programmes of study and the NNS assertion that the work should be connected.

The secondary Framework does not offer week-by-week objectives, which allows more opportunity to develop the mathematics. The timings seem prescriptive, but they can be adapted to suit: 'Good planning ensures that mathematical ideas are presented in an interrelated way, not in isolation from each other. Awareness of the connections helps pupils to make sense of the subject, avoid misconceptions and retain what they learn' (DfEE 2001: 1/46).

The interrelation of topics can lead to the learner having the opportunity to come to know things better. By making connections and working in a variety of contexts, the curriculum can become smaller to manage. You have to decide on the best ways for your learners to progress. Delivering content to prescription may account for the curriculum. Putting the learning first may help pupils to know the mathematics better. Departments will have to decide how much of their medium-term planning they will adapt as they consider the demands of the Framework.

The following description of lesson planning will not be unfamiliar:

> Short-term or lesson plans are the teaching notes for a block of lessons. They show how a unit of work will unfold to meet the intended objectives. They indicate objectives for each lesson or group of lessons that form part of the unit, outline starter activities, show how work will be developed in the main part of the lessons through teaching input and pupil activities, indicate how lessons will be rounded off and suggest what homework will be set. (1/44)

Teachers have always planned in this way, devising activities and deciding on timings and sequences. 'The main requirement of a short-term plan is that it makes clear how the objectives for the relevant unit will be taught' (1/44). The new responsibility is in the detail of the objectives and you will need to balance the need to account for coverage with the needs of your learners.

Analysing part of the teaching programme

There is no advice in any of the documents on how to move from the teaching aims to the learning outcomes, other than by inference. There is little advice on what you have to teach the pupils in order that they can be assessed using a particular assessment item from the examples in Section 4. Practising the assessment item alone is not good teaching, although it might provide good assessment results in the short term. Progression through the mathematics needs to be determined to suit the learner. Learning experiences have to be created for particular classes and particular needs. This, quite rightly, is the job of the skilled professional.

The teaching programmes offer objectives from Year 7 to Year 9 and it seems sensible to analyse the curriculum for the lower years with an eye on the higher years, to maintain continuity. This can help to define progression within the mathematics. It may not, however, offer a teaching order, but given that it defines what will be assessed at the end of Year 9, it can help with this.

Table 2.6 Construction and loci objectives from Section 4

Section 4	Year 7	Year 8	Year 9
220	Construct lines, angles and shapes		
224		Find simple loci by reasoning and by using ICT	

Let us consider the construction and loci strand from the Framework. Firstly, Table 2.6 shows the objectives from Section 4, which tells about this strand across the Key Stage.

It seems manageable so far! Table 2.7 is taken from the detail of the yearly programme objectives for the construction and loci strands. You may already have a good sense of the construction objectives in Table 2.6, but you will need to check the particular interpretation of the Framework. Here you will read a renewed emphasis on knowing about the construction of triangles given certain conditions. Table 2.7 shows the objectives from Section 3.

The Year 9 key extension objective offers a clue to the progression implied by the Framework: 'know from experience of constructing them that triangles given SSS, SAS, ASA or RHS are unique, but that triangles given SSA are not' (DfEE 2000b: 3/11).

Table 2.7 The yearly teaching programmes, construction and loci

Example pages	Year 7 Revision of Level 4, but mainly Level 5	Year 8 Consolidation of Level 5, start on Level 6	Year 9 Revision of Level 5, but mainly Level 6
220–27	**Construction**	**Construction and loci**	
220–23	Use a ruler and protractor to: • measure and draw lines to the nearest mm and angles, including reflex angles to the nearest degree • construct a triangle given SAS or ASA. Explore these constructions using ICT.	**Use a straight edge and compasses to construct:** • **the midpoint and perpendicular bisector of a line segment** • **the bisector of an angle** • **the perpendicular from a point to a line** • **the perpendicular from a point on a line.** Construct a triangle given SSS. Use ICT to explore these constructions.	Use a straight edge and compasses to construct a triangle, given a right angle, hypotenuse and side (RHS). Use ICT to explore constructions of triangles and other 2D shapes.
222–3	Use a ruler and protractor to construct simple nets of 3D shapes, e.g. cuboid, regular tetrahedron, square-based pyramid, triangular prism.		
221			*Know from experience of constructing them that triangles given SSS, SAS, ASA or RHS are unique, but that triangles given SSA or AAA are not.*
224–7		Find simple loci, both by reasoning and by using ICT, to produce shapes and paths, e.g. an equilateral triangle.	Find the locus of an object moving according to a simple rule, both by reasoning and by using ICT. *Extend to more complex rules involving loci and simple constructions.*

Objectives in bold are key objectives; italics are Year 9 for able pupils.

In Year 7, pupils are expected to construct triangles given SAS or ASA, Year 8 given SSS and Year 9 given RHS. There is no mention of SSA, nor is there mention of the AAA triangle, which can offer a lot of practice in measuring angles. The complete set of SSS, SAS, ASA, RHS, SSA and AAA are not mentioned until the objectives for Year 9 able pupils. A teaching syllabus will need to consider all the constructions of congruent and similar triangles with the appropriate language. It will also need to ensure that pupils see the connections between the different types of triangles and the implications for uniqueness and definition.

When you look closely at the objectives you will notice aspects that make you think about their roles. The objective for constructing nets in Year 7 seems a wasted opportunity, as presumably pupils are not expected to use the different constructions given in Year 8. The objective in Year 8 using loci to produce shapes would seem to be an ideal way of constructing nets. Nets could also be a useful context for exploring triangles, for example in finding nets of triangular prisms. So the objective from Year 7 can be revisited purposefully in Year 8.

Making connections

There is no doubt that you will teach a topic on constructions during Year 7, but in fact it is the connections (see Figures 2.1, 2.1, 2.3 and 2.4) that give purpose to using the ruler and protractor. Constructing triangles can appear purposeless, unless you are exploring whether or not the information is sufficient to get everyone to produce the same diagram or to explore the angles, congruence or similarity. Exploring loci, constructing nets or symmetrical shapes in an interrelated way, can make the mathematics more memorable and offers purpose, and can reduce the amount of work in the syllabus.

In Figures 2.1, 2.2 and 2.3 we have connected some of the mathematics given for each of the years using the construction and loci objectives. The figures show some of the appropriate content. In Figure 2.4 we have connected them all because the individual diagrams suggested links.

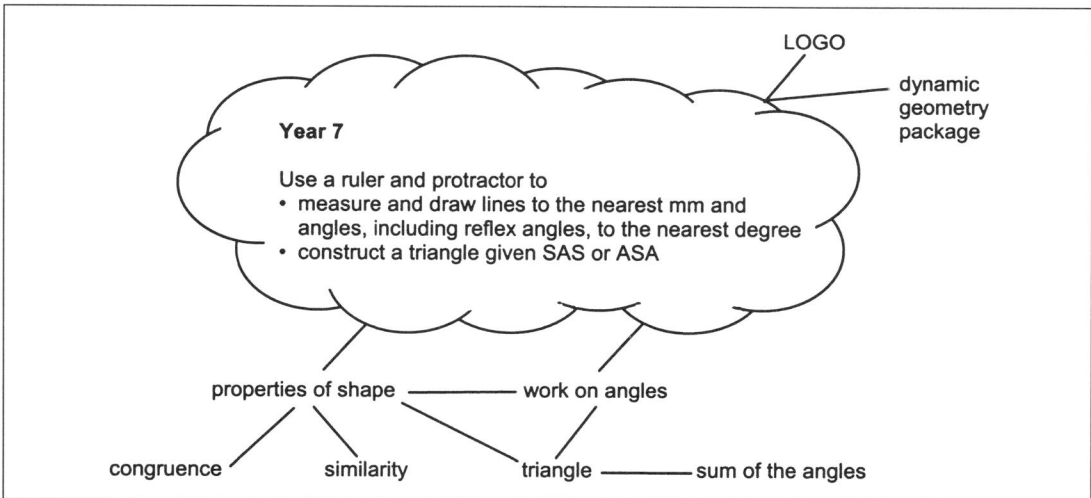

Figure 2.1 Splurge diagram of the Year 7 construction objective

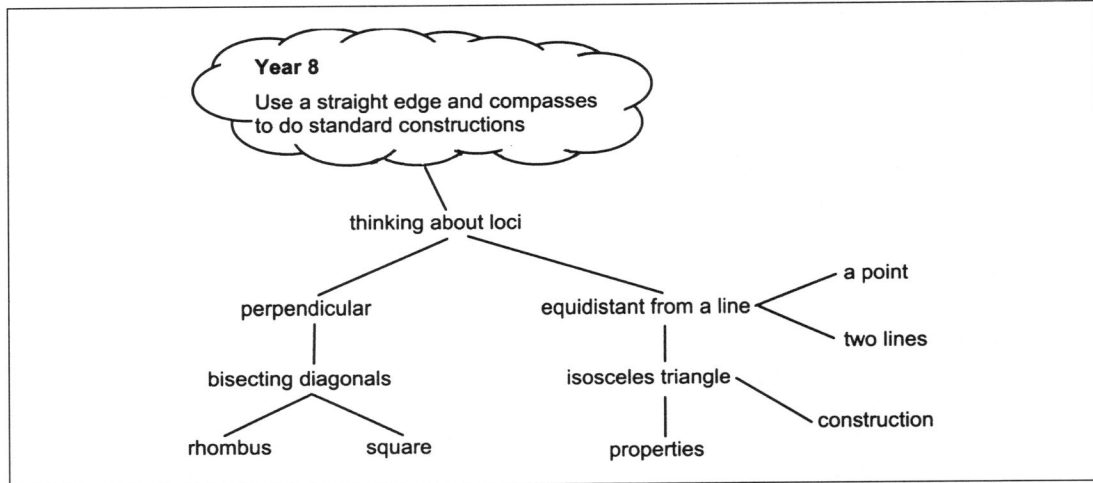

Figure 2.2 Splurge diagram of the Year 8 construction objective

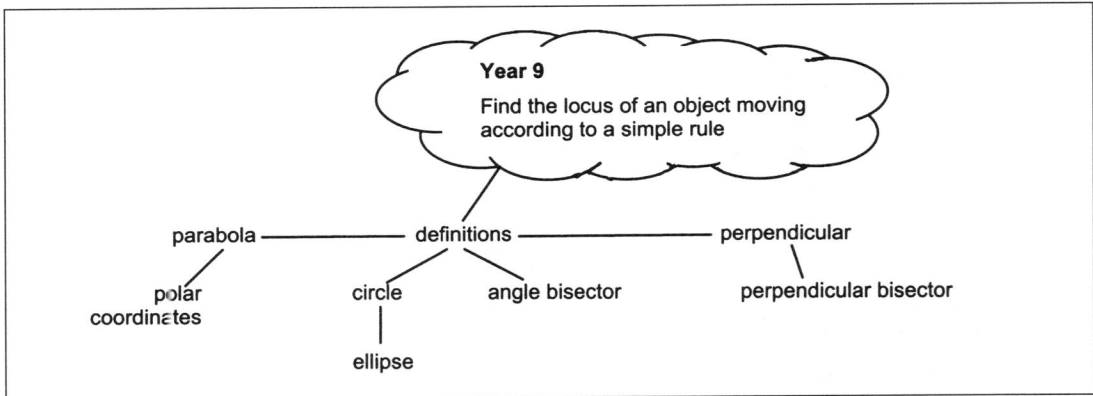

Figure 2.3 Splurge diagram of the Year 9 locus objective

Figure 2.4 may look complicated but it gives a sense of how much content can be linked by these three objectives. We began with three separate splurges, which were then linked. You may want to try this for yourself before you look more closely at Figure 2.4. There are other ways of thinking about the connections. If you work on diagrams like this you will put the words in different orders and different links, as would we if drawing them at another time. The links also highlight the opportunities for revisiting the content. The language of dynamic geometry packages matches the labels for constructions. Using circles to obtain triangles with given lengths reinforces the definition of the locus of the triangle. The parabola can be defined as a locus (points equidistant from a point and a line) as well as the familiar quadratic equation. The diagram may seem fussy, but it can simplify the mathematics by stressing connections.

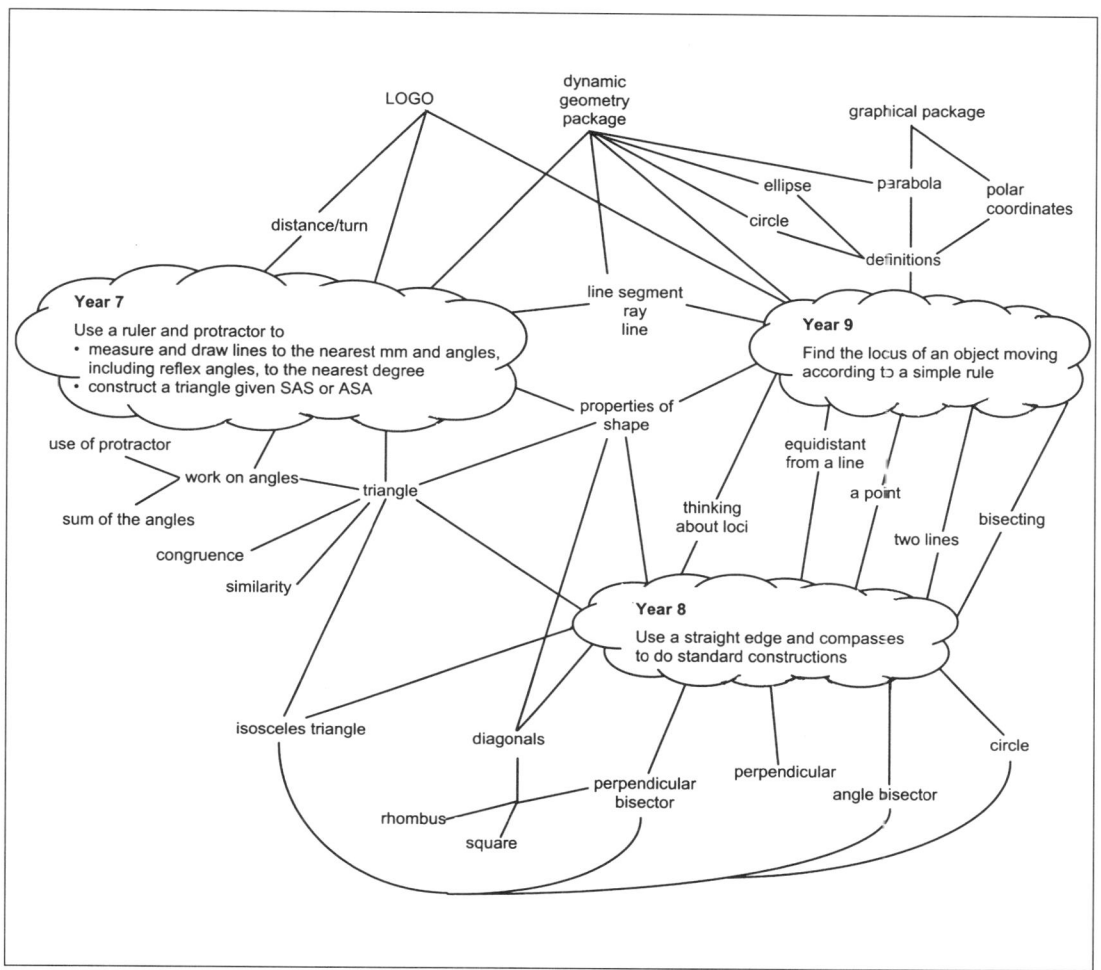

Figure 2.4 Splurge diagram connecting Years 7–9 objectives

Summary

The NNS offers a reworking of the National Curriculum with a return to more detail and more prescription. In this chapter we have considered the language of objectives, key objectives and units of work. We have found it useful to think of planning using key objectives and the Years 7–9 objectives given in the Framework examples (more of that in Chapter 8) and at the end of this chapter we offer tables for the other strands to show the connections across the years. You may find it simpler to work to Tables 2.8–2.25 than using the presentation in the Framework document.

The language of objectives is very familiar to us, but remember that teaching objectives do not imply learning outcomes. We can plan to teach but then observe whether or not learning happens, and then readjust the planning. Units of work may recommend hours of teaching, but there is no point in racing through a curriculum if pupils are failing to learn. Of course the arrival at the end of a 'unit' may come as a relief if the topic is meaning nothing to the pupils. Use the recommendations, if you possibly can, as a guide to your planning.

Objectives from the supplement of examples, Section 4

Numbers and the number system

Table 2.8 Place value, ordering and rounding

	Year 7	Year 8	Year 9
36	Understand and use decimal notation and place value; multiply and divide positive integers and decimals by a power of 10		
40	Compare and order decimals		
42	Round number		
46			. . . including significant figures

Table 2.9 Integers, powers and roots

	Year 7	Year 8	Year 9
48	Order, add, subtract, multiply and divide positive and negative integers		
52	Recognise and use multiples, factors and primes; use tests of divisibility		
56	Recognise squares and cubes and the corresponding roots; use index notation		

Table 2.10 Fractions, decimals, percentages, ratio, proportion

	Year 7	Year 8	Year 9
60	Use fraction notation; recognise and use the equivalence of fractions and decimals		
66	Calculate fractions of quantities; add, subtract, multiply and divide fractions		
70	Understand percentages; recognise equivalences; calculate percentages		
78	Understand the relationship between ratio and proportion		

Calculations

Table 2.11 Number operations and relationships between them

	Year 7	Year 8	Year 9
82	Understand the relationship between multiplication and division; know the laws of arithmetic		
86	Know and use the order of operations, including brackets		

Table 2.12 Mental methods and rapid recall of number facts

	Year 7	Year 8	Year 9
88	Consolidate rapid recall of number facts		
92	Consolidate and extend mental methods of calculation		
102	Make and justify estimates and approximations		

Table 2.13 Written methods

	Year 7	Year 8	Year 9
104	Use efficient column methods for addition and subtraction; extend to decimals		
104	Refine written methods of multiplication and division; extend to decimals		

Table 2.14 Calculator methods

	Year 7	Year 8	Year 9
108	Carry out more complex calculations using the facilities on a calculator		
110	Use checking procedures		

Algebra

Table 2.15 (2.4 repeated) Equations, formulae and identities

S. 4	Year 7	Year 8	Year 9
112	Use letter symbols and distinguish their different roles in algebra		
114	Know BODMAS and use index notation and laws		
116	Simplify or transform algebraic expressions		
122	Construct and solve linear equations, selecting an appropriate method		
126			Solve a pair of simultaneous linear equations
130		Solve linear inequalities in one variable, begin to solve in two variables	
132			Use systematic trial and improvement
136		Solve problems involving direct proportion	
138	Use formulae		

Table 2.16 (2.5 repeated) Sequences, functions and graphs

S. 4	Year 7	Year 8	Year 9
144	Generate and describe sequences		
148	Generate sequences using term-to-term and position-to-term definitions		
154	Find the nth term		
160	Express functions and represent mappings		
164	Generate points and plot graphs of functions		
172	Construct functions arising from real-life situations		

Shape, space and measures

Table 2.17 Geometrical reasoning: lines, angles and shapes

	Year 7	Year 8	Year 9
178	Use accurately vocabulary, notation and labelling conventions; distinguish between conventions, facts, definitions and derived properties		
180	Identify properties of angles and parallel and perpendicular lines		
184	Identify and use the geometric properties of triangles, quadrilaterals and other polygons; explain and justify inferences and deductions using mathematics reasoning		
190		Understand congruence and similarity	
194			Identify and use properties of circles
198	Use 2D representations to visualise 3D shapes		

Table 2.18 Transformations

	Year 7	Year 8	Year 9
202	Understand and use the language and notation associated with reflections, rotations and transformations. Recognise and visualise transformations and symmetries of 2D shapes		
216		Use and interpret maps and scale drawings	

Table 2.19 Coordinates

	Year 7	Year 8	Year 9
218	Use coordinates in all four quadrants		

Table 2.20 Construction and loci

	Year 7	Year 8	Year 9
220	Construct lines, angles and shapes		
224		Find simple loci by reasoning and by using ICT	

Table 2.21 Measures and mensuration

	Year 7	Year 8	Year 9
228	Know and use units of measurement to measure, estimate and solve problems, convert between units and know rough metric equivalents of common imperial units		
232	Extend the range of measures to angle measure and bearings and compound measures		
234	Deduce and use formulae to calculate lengths, perimeters, areas and volumes in 2D and 3D shapes		
242			Begin to use sine, cosine and tangent

Handling data

Table 2.22 Specifying a problem, planning and collecting data

	Year 7	Year 8	Year 9
248	Discuss a problem that can be addressed by statistical methods		
250	Identify which data to collect and identify possible sources		
252	Plan to collect data and organise the data		

Table 2.23 Processing and representing data

	Year 7	Year 8	Year 9
256	Calculate statistics, using ICT as appropriate		
262	Construct graphs and diagrams to represent data		

Table 2.24 Interpreting and discussing results

	Year 7	Year 8	Year 9
268	Interpret diagrams and graphs and draw inferences		
272	Compare two distributions using the range, mean, median or mode		
274	Communicate methods and results		

Table 2.25 Probability

	Year 7	Year 8	Year 9
276	Use the vocabulary of probability		
278	Use the probability scale, find and justify theoretical probabilities		
282	Collect and record experimental data, estimate probabilities		
284	Compare experimental and theoretical probabilities		

3 Advice for teaching

In this chapter we will look at the advice in Section 1, pages 26–38, of the Framework (DfEE 2001), which considers the teaching of mathematics, lesson structures and inclusion. The Framework presents advice mainly about curriculum content (what to teach) but there is some input on pedagogy and structure (how to teach). Already there is a great deal of folklore arising from the proposals for 'whole-class teaching' and the 'three-part lesson'. Debates about attainment have been fuelled by the performance of English students in international studies such as the Third International Mathematics and Science Study (TIMSS). The national strategy for mathematics deliberately sought influences from curricula from abroad. Browr et al. (2000) trace the context of influence for the NNS, including the Kassell project, which looked at comparisons with other countries (Burghes 1999), and a report commissioned by the Chief Inspector for Schools, which included suggestions for whole-class teaching from Taiwan, three-part lessons from Japan and undifferentiated curricula from Hungary (Reynolds and Farrell 1996). All of these have influenced the NNS. All of these have also been picked up by the media, thrown into a melting pot and recreated to suit the latest spin. The results will no doubt become orthodoxy for school practices and eventually be looked for in classrooms by inspectors

Meanwhile, in the context of regular inspection, certain freedoms are deceptive and there is heavy pressure on schools and departments to conform. We will not offer much research detail in this book but there is plenty to be found if you need support for arguments to governing bodies. For example, the use of undifferentiated curricula from Hungary is set within a completely different teaching and learning and social culture (Hatch 1999) and there is no clear evidence that whole-class teaching is more effective:

> In spite of the claims of the Task Force that 'there is support in the research for an association between more successful teaching of numeracy and a higher proportion of whole class teaching' (DfEE, 1998, p. 19), the evidence is not unambiguous. It depends mostly on large-scale studies which cannot easily establish causation and can only report variables that are measurable.
>
> (Brown *et al.* 1988: 370)

Be aware of mixed messages. You will need to balance the demands of OFSTED, whole-school policies, departmental needs and your own interpretations of policies and what is best for your pupils. Prescriptions about content can be enforced by the demands of external examinations. Prescriptions about teaching never work. Such prescriptions assume that all classes are the same, that all teachers work in the same way and that all classrooms work to order. You may work to the prescriptions at particular moments in the year and school policy documents must reflect current government policy. Professional critical intelligence can be used to explain and justify actions and interpretations.

Direct teaching

The section in the Framework on 'direct teaching' has echoes of the very influential Cockcroft Report (1982), which listed lesson ingredients (paragraph 243). Of direct teaching the Framework suggests, 'Aim to spend a high proportion of time of each lesson on direct teaching, often of the whole class but also of groups and individuals' (DfEE 2000b: 1/23). But what is the explanation of 'direct' teaching in the document?

> High-quality direct teaching is oral, interactive and lively and will not be achieved by lecturing the class, or by always expecting all pupils to teach themselves indirectly from books. It is a two-way process in which pupils are expected to play an active part by answering questions, contributing to discussions, and explaining and demonstrating their methods and solutions to others in the class.   (DfEE 2001: 1/26)

This requires consideration. The 'good' teacher, the effective teacher, is far more sophisticated than this and will deliberately include silent lessons, reading lessons, and research lessons, as well as a substantial amount of indirect teaching, such as playing games in which the learning of mathematics is subordinated to the activity to great effect. Also, if the long-term aim of teaching is to help pupils to become more and more independent in their own learning and in their ability to make and monitor choices (as required to satisfy Ma1) then the teacher cannot go on 'directing' forever. The teacher will direct in order not to direct, but more of that later.

Meanwhile let's explore the elements of 'good direct teaching', which the Framework (p. 26–7) suggests requires a balance of:

- directing and telling
- demonstrating and modelling
- explaining and illustrating
- questioning and discussing
- exploring and investigating
- consolidating and embedding
- reflecting and evaluating
- summarising and reminding.

The list contains elements that would be part of the teaching strategies of every teacher. However, this is not a list defined in the research literature. Nor would you find agreement on the difference between, let's say, directing and demonstrating, or demonstrating and explaining. We need to be critical of the influence of such lists.

> Since the documents also freely use with approval words like 'instruction', 'direct teaching', 'effective questioning' and the Framework refers to large numbers of fragmented procedures, there are risks that many teachers may perceive the Numeracy Strategy as being supportive of a more traditional 'transmission' style. Askew *et al.* (1997) found that low numeracy gains were obtained by transmission

approaches, where teachers demonstrated specific procedures, often preceded by practical and/or diagrammatic justifications. (Brown *et al.* 1988: 373)

So it's not just a case of doing the list: it's not what you do, it's the way that you do it! It would be worthwhile deciding for yourself the meaning of these words and maybe the meaning intended by the document. We offer our interpretations below.

The words actually serve different purposes in the classroom: some are teaching acts, which are planned for a lesson; some are teaching acts used during the lesson to respond to a particular moment; and some fulfil both purposes. You might like to draw your own diagram for these words (see Figure 3.1).

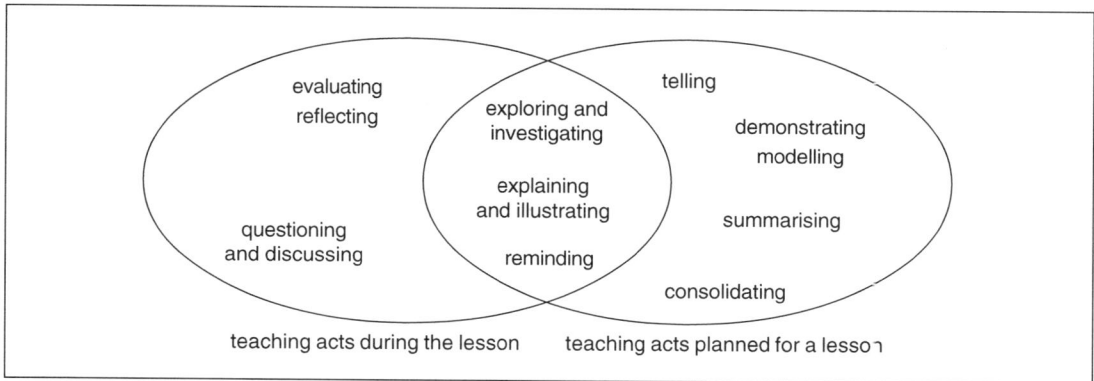

Figure 3.1 Connecting the elements of direct teaching

The problem with lists is that they can seem to be definitive, which is, clearly, not possible. Teaching is much more than lists. You might explore what has *not* been included. We will consider the notion of balance later in this chapter via the infinite number of professional choices that you will make before and during a lesson. The main reason for looking at these words is that knowing about them will make you better prepared to answer questions from outsiders. It is also valuable to know the alternatives for your own teaching:

A pedagogic act involves those who are teaching in informed interpretations of learners, knowledge and environments in order to manipulate environments in ways which help learners make sense of the knowledge available to them. It is an intense, complex and discursive act which demands considerable expertise. (Edwards 2000: 5)

Demonstrating and modelling

giving clear, well-structured demonstrations ... modelling mathematics using appropriate resources and visual displays (DfEE 2001: 1/26)

This includes demonstrating mathematical concepts and new ideas, and finding ways to provoke understanding for pupils. Of course, there is a range of 'why', 'what' and 'how':

- Demonstrate *why* something is so:
- use ICT to show that the angle in a semi-circle is always 90 degrees;
- use a visual aid to show that the square on the hypotenuse of a right-angled triangle is equal to the sum of the squares on the other two sides.

- Demonstrate *what* something is:
  - walk along the path of a polygon, showing the external angles;
  - follow pupils' instructions to draw a shape.
- Demonstrate *how* to do something:
  - how to use a protractor;
  - how to draw a line of best fit.

Explaining and illustrating

> giving accurate, well paced explanations, and referring to previous work or methods
>
> (DfEE 2001: 1/27)

Here is another tautologous definition. We are not sure why referencing back is the only context given in the definition. Maybe the question to ask here is about 'accurate and well paced': well paced for whom? How would you judge success and measure accuracy and pace?

Questioning and discussing

> questioning in ways which match the direction and pace of the lesson to ensure that all pupils take part.
>
> (DfEE 2001: 1/27)

This is definitely the crux of good teaching! The advice in this section is apt and offers thoughts about relationships and communications in the classroom. This section could be a permanent feature on a departmental meeting agenda as it involves much more than the teacher asking a question, the class putting up their hands and then the teacher selecting a pupil to answer. How do you ensure that all pupils take part and are affirmed in your classroom? What is a 'good' question from a pupil? What is a good answer? What are the types of questions you might ask?

Working on questions is a good activity for departments. You might find the book *Questions and Prompts for Mathematical Thinking* (Watson and Mason 1998) useful to start discussions.

Exploring and investigating

> Asking pupils to pose problems or suggest a line of enquiry . . . to seek counter-examples . . . to move from one form to another to gain different perspectives on the problem
>
> (DfEE 2001: 1/27)

This section describes many of the processes in Ma1, Using and Applying Mathematics, in the National Curriculum. It is also valuable in reminding mathematics departments of how they can work on thinking skills. Its inclusion, as part of the strategies for 'good direct teaching', offers an encouraging balance to the more didactic sections in the list. Building in aspects of Ma1 to the main part of the lesson allows a movement towards the independent learner, where posing questions can be as important as solving them, where alternative methods can be valued and the processes of mathematics become as valid as answers.

Consolidating and embedding

> providing varied opportunities to practise and develop newly learned skills
>
> (DfEE 2001: 1/27)

You might want to consolidate for a part of a lesson or a whole lesson depending on your evaluation of the previous lesson and learning. In this respect, if the curriculum has been well constructed, developing what has been taught is a permanent feature of good teaching. Suggestions are given about paired discussion on what happened in the lesson. This is a good strategy for establishing discussion, which itself often promotes learning. The activity of paired discussion is more about the opportunity for the pupils to talk through the mathematics and is a crucial part of any learning process rather than only for consolidation. It does not, however, seem to fit the overall definition of direct teaching. Perhaps this is where 'directing' comes in. Paired (or group) discussion will not happen if the material is not suitable to discussion, if the participants are not used to discussion or if one person tries to force their view on others. The good teacher will balance the needs of individuals with appropriate content, practice in discussion and intervention when necessary.

Reflecting and evaluating

> identifying pupils' erors , using them as positive teaching points by talking about them
>
> (DfEE 2001: 1/27)

This connects to the previous section about asking questions and listening to responses and then responding appropriately. Good teachers know how to listen, and act on what they hear. These teaching skills are part of the informal assessment done in every lesson. You evaluate pupil responses, both spoken and written, to judge the learning and to adapt your teaching.

Summarising and reminding

> reviewing during and towards the end of a lesson the mathematics that has been taught and what pupils have learned
>
> (DfEE 2001: 1/27)

Again, the timing of this teacher act must be in response to what is happening in the lesson. If the learning does not take place as expected you could not 'do' a planned summary, but during a lesson a good teacher will pick up opportunities to confirm the mathematics for the pupils. The issue may be who does the summary. A summary given by the teacher may not be as effective as pupils working on their own descriptions of the mathematics.

Directing and telling

We would use this category for telling about the givens in mathematics such as plotting a coordinate point, and how to construct coordinate axes. The examples given in the Framework for this category (describing how to solve an algebraic equation, how to interpret a graph) would be better under another heading, since understanding is paramount for sustained knowing, for interpreting and developing a mathematical argument. (But you can see that we are already meeting the problem of using discrete definitions. These definitions are useful for departmental discussion and provoking thinking about action but not for improving pedagogy.)

Finally we would like to consider the work 'directing', which was offered at the top of the list to explain about good teaching. The Framework explains directing as 'sharing your teaching objectives with the class' (DfEE 2001: 1/26). It is time to stand up and say 'No, not always!' It all depends. If you look back in history there are different types of teachers and hence teaching styles. Here are three:

- *The Socratic method* Socrates was renowned for his skills as a teacher. The Socratic method of teaching was to engage by questioning. The questions were very directed, leading to a goal that the teacher knew but the pupil had to discern by the end of the dialogue.
- *The Rabbinical method* The most famous rabbinical teacher was probably Jesus. He would teach about values and morals through stories and parables. He did not declare his teaching objectives first but wove them through his stories. His storytelling can hook you into the moral so that the learning lasts longer.
- *The newsreader* Modern day newsreaders deliver the news in a three-part structure. First they tell you what the news is (bong), then they tell you in detail about the news (bong) and then they tell you what they have just told you, summarising the news (bong). I need only store the information in my short-term memory because, if I wish, I can hear it again in an hour's time. Or I may go and find out more about a particular part of the news, or tell it to someone else, and then I begin to remember it better.

You might use any of these styles at any time in your teaching. You will choose what is most appropriate for your audience. Maybe the idea of directing could be that of the theatre director, who sometimes gives very detailed instructions, sometimes gives the actors complete freedom to interpret the material, and sometimes uses a style somewhere in between the two. Sometimes the rehearsal will begin with a warm-up, an improvisation say, but sometimes it might pick up from where it was left yesterday. Like the great directors, the good teacher has a range of skills that will be recreated and balanced anew in every lesson.

Lesson styles and structures

What occurs in the classroom is ordinary and familiar. The result is dramatic. The cumulative effect of everyday classroom experiences is similar to that of falling snow. No single snowflake or lesson makes an obvious difference; the cumulative effect is undeniable. Further, as those who dwell in the colder regions can attest, 'snow' is not simply 'snow'. Different types of snow yield qualitatively different effects. Tiny, dry, sparkling snowflakes can be effortlessly swept away. Large, moist, heavy flakes cling to branches and require great effort to move. Lessons similarly differ qualitatively in how curriculum and pedagogy are woven together. (Schmidt *et al.* 1996: 2)

Some people write about effective teaching in a clinical prescriptive way. They imply that there are teaching rules that are easy to follow, with certain outcomes (Reynolds 1998). You only have to look back over the past century to know that teaching and learning are not simply achieved, that weaving curriculum and pedagogy in different ways can have dramatic effects and that what works for one teacher cannot be aped by another. Schmidt *et al.* continue to say that one explanation is that teaching and what is taught is fundamentally embedded in culture (which is why we cannot transport whole strategies from Taiwan, Hungary or Japan). They are discussing the differences across six countries but it is also true of different classroom cultures within a country. How you choose to construct and plan for learning will depend on the time of day, the age of the class, the layout of the classroom and the mathematics you want to work on. So the aspects of your teaching will vary. Different styles of teaching will have different effects. Different sorts of directing bring out different performances from individual actors. Here is a description of a Japanese lesson (with no oral/mental starter!):

> a fairly consistent lesson structure [in Japan] – what might be labelled problem-oriented teaching. Lessons began with the presentation of the problem or situation. Discussion was then used to help students generate ideas and approaches to the problem or situation . . . . [groups then worked on the problem] This was followed by general discussion of ideas and solutions subtly directed by the teacher. The general discussion ended with a succinct summary by the teacher at the lesson's end.
>
> (Schmidt *et al.* 1996: 94)

The advice in the Framework on lesson structure is not consistent except for a lesson in three parts. It starts on page 28 with the following:

> The outline structure of the three-part lesson described below is highly recommended since it can be adapted to different circumstances. It provides a 'beginning, a middle and an end' in which you explain to pupils what they are to learn, and prepare them for what they are to learn, teach it to them, then help them to recognise what they have achieved.
>
> (DfEE 2001: 1/28)

This particular piece of advice follows a single 'type' of lesson (in the newsreader style):

- tell the pupils the objectives and learning outcomes of the lesson;
- teach explicitly for particular learning outcomes;
- relate the teaching to the given objectives to identify potential learning.

This model assumes much about learning, but mainly that teaching and learning are directly related, which is not always the case. The quote also implies that the three parts of the lesson are explicitly connected. However, on page 28 the three parts recommended are:

- an oral and mental starter
- the main teaching activity
- a plenary.

Here the descriptions of oral and mental starters indicate activities that may or may not be connected to the main teaching activity. The choice belongs to the teacher: 'This outline is not a mechanistic recipe to be followed. Use your professional judgement to determine the activities, timing and organisation of the beginning, middle and end of the lesson to suit its objectives' (DfEE 2001: 1/28).

We have no objections to three-part lessons, but the Framework does offer a limited and unsophisticated view of a lesson structure. Elsewhere, we have used the analogy of eating a three-course meal to consider the teaching of the three-part lesson (Prestage and Perks 2001). The comparison is immediate. We don't want to eat three-course meals every day, and nor do we want to teach three-part lessons every day; it can be too much. We might prefer to linger over the starter; we are often too full for the pudding if we have a starter and a main course; is the third part of the meal coffee, cheese and biscuits, a sumptuous pudding or a share of two or more puddings? We like to vary the style of our food intake, and so too do we like to vary our learning and the structure of the lessons we teach.

This does not mean that we do not recommend three-part lessons, in whatever form. Our pupils need to be used to Framework three-part lessons, as we would hope they are used to eating three-course meals. We want them to be used to eating three-course meals so that when we take them to a restaurant or to eat with their grandparents (to extend the analogy, for grandparents read OFSTED inspectors) they can cope with the cutlery. Sometimes, however, we would like a seven-course meal, or a buffet, or soup in a cup, or just a pudding! So we would like variety in our lessons. Here are two different structures for you to think about.

The buffet

This style of lesson is based on choice and a circus of activities exploring the same mathematics offering different approaches to suit different learners. The example given is for work on solving equations intended for consolidation and practice sessions.

Equations circus

Card game: Matching equation and solution cards.

Card game: Matching expression, number and solution cards.

Board game Move according to the solution of the equation.

Worksheet: Matching equations with solutions.

Worksheet: Solving equations.

Graphical calculators: Solving simultaneous equations.

The buffet style also represents differentiation by choice. The tasks, short or long can be chosen by the pupils to suit their own perceived needs. How does the list for direct teaching fit this lesson style?

A sandwich

This represents a three-part lesson where the first and third parts are of the same form for work on multiplication tables.

Part 1: Oral practice of the seven times table, noticing hesitancy.

Part 2: Using a calculator and the constant to generate the seven, seventeen, and twenty-seven times tables. Look at the patterns in the units digits. Write down as many patterns as you can.

Part 3: Oral practice of the seven times table, noticing hesitancy. Has anything changed?

There are many other styles. You choose according to the content, the learners and even the time of day. Use of the three-part lesson should be an intellectual choice made because it is best for the particular lesson.

Inclusion and differentiation with undifferentiated curricula

> The National Numeracy Strategy was established in 1998, with an ambitious target: that 75% of 11-year-olds achieve at least level 4 in the National Curriculum tests by the year 2002. . . . The challenge now is to secure and build on . . . [those] achievements . . . The National Strategy for Key Stage 3 aims to address this challenge . . . The Government intends to set ambitious targets for achievement in the National Curriculum tests for mathematics by 2007, with a milestone target for 2004.   (DfEE 2001: 1/2)

Whatever the context of influence on the policy of the Framework, the expectation of high average achievement is a major political thrust of the policy and one that has huge implications for mathematics departments. The majority of pupils in Year 7 are expected to work at Level 5 with an undifferentiated curriculum. School departments will have to create appropriate and sensible teaching sequences for all pupils at KS3 that match appropriate learning needs and that also account for the expected coverage of the Framework. The use of the appalling phrase coined for the below average pupil – those who must play 'catch-up' (p. 1/34) – needs attention. The competitive macho speeding through the curriculum for the above average pupil also needs to be considered for its appropriateness. There is no doubt that these two areas will be of major importance.

Can this policy significantly shift the attainment of the past century? Who knows. Even if the NNS sees primary pupils reaching the politically defined goals in 2002, this still means that 25 per cent of pupils coming into secondary schools (and special schools) will have SATs results lower than Level 4.

The National Curriculum offers three very useful headings for inclusion, which summarise most of what departments need to consider: 'Setting suitable learning challenges: Responding to pupils' diverse learning needs: Overcoming potential barriers to learning and assessment for individuals and groups of pupils' (DfEE 1999: 74). There is lots of sensible, pertinent advice to be found in these sections of the National Curriculum and you may find support here for action that your department might take, especially if you feel it inappropriate to offer every pupil Level 5 work:

> Teachers should teach the knowledge, skills and understanding in ways that suit their pupils' abilities. This may mean choosing knowledge, skills and understanding from earlier or later key stages so that individual pupils can make progress and show what they can achieve.
> (DfEE 1999: p 74)

The Framework section on inclusion (DfEE 2001: 1/32–8) follows similar ideas. Two major ideas in this section, 'Pupils who are very able' and 'Pupils who need to catch up', are discussed below. Some other headings, probably already reflected in departmental policies, are quoted for you to check against your own policies.

Pupils with difficulties in reading or writing: Remember that mathematics has a strong visual element and capitalise on this wherever you can to illuminate meaning ... Make frequent use of visual aids such as number lines, place value charts, ... computer software ... and games and puzzles where the rules are picked up quickly by watching a demonstration. Use games and activities with familiar rules ... like Bingo and Countdown. (1/35)

Pupils learning English as an additional language (EAL): In oral work, it may help to use extra visual clues or gestures, or translation. Use picture cues on written materials and simplify the words, but not the mathematics. ... Peer-group talk helps pupils to make sense of and apply mathematical ideas. (1/35)

Pupils who are working well below the national expectations for their year group: You may need to refer to the teaching programmes for Key Stage 2 or Key Stage 1, modifying the ideas to set them in a context suited to 11- to 14-year-old pupils. ... Some pupils may be working at pre-level 1 for much of their secondary education. QCA intends to publish curriculum guidelines for pupils whose attainment by the age of 16 is expected to remain within the range from pre-level 1 to level 2. Challenging mathematics targets for these pupils may be found in the earliest stages of the primary Framework. (1/37)

We now turn our attention to the sections 'Pupils who are very able' and 'Pupils who need to catch up'. Neither of these descriptions of pupils, extremes of the range, will be new to teachers working within the comprehensive system and it may be that your department already has a perfectly acceptable working policy, curriculum and teaching programme.

Pupils who are very able

There are those who are able, there are those who are very able and there are those who are gifted. Such differences seem to exist more blatantly in subjects like mathematics, music and art, and different schools have different ways of ensuring appropriate challenges. The Framework suggest that able pupils can be stretched by:

- harder problems and extra challenges;
- differentiated group work;
- working on topics from the teaching programme for older pupils.

Most secondary teachers and departments already have access to a range of 'harder' questions for pupils, since many of the topics in the secondary school mathematics curriculum recycle across the age groups. Differentiated work is always necessary to provide extra challenges.

One suggestion that is often offered for brighter pupils is to accelerate them through the curriculum. The Framework suggests using the next year's programme. Certainly, the next year's programme may offer suitable contexts for all pupils to work on, and in a setted situation such management decisions may be possible (although this brings its own problems of movement between sets). However, there are some objectives from the higher years that might be sensible for all Year 7 pupils to work on. For example consider 'make and justify estimates and approximations of calculations', a Year 9 key objective. All pupils should be working on this from Year 7; it is an essential aspect of calculation. So although it is a key objective for Year 9 and will be assessed at the end of the Key Stage, it is suitable content for all secondary pupils. As for other forms of acceleration, we do question the validity of pupils racing through the curriculum just to do examinations early. A recent repcrt, compiled by a group representing all sections concerned with the mathematics education of able youngsters concluded that 'The policy [the DfEE's Gifted and talented programme] is being developed in a way which ignores what we know about the development of able youngsters and is likely to damage a whole generation of talent' (Gardiner 2000). This report argues against collecting examinations and modules at the expense of depth. Racing to an examination may occupy these pupils, but working on some challenging mathematics problems would probably be a better preparation for A-level mathematics and keep some of the most able interested in the subject after the age of 16. In fact a good idea for your bright pupils might be to work with the standard core of the curriculum content for the age group but require deeper understanding of the material. Building in lots of Ma1 processes with plenty of decision-making, justification and proof would also create opportunity for greater depth in the standard topics (this is similar to the Hungarian teaching approach).

Pupils who need to catch up: working with pupils who have not achieved Level 4

'Catch-up' is perhaps the most offensive phrase in the Framework document, denying dignity to those pupils who are working and attaining to the best of their ability at KS2 but who have not achieved Level 4. With the phrase 'catch-up' the policy deliberately constructs failure. It is for these pupils that departments will have to plan most carefully as they implement the Framework. Although many schools will work with mixed ability pupils in the first year of secondary schools, many do set their pupils at some stage (although if you need some arguments for not setting, read Boaler *et al.* 2000). This simplifies the management of a differentiated curriculum for pupils with different levels of achievement. The Framework, however, expects the majority of pupils to work on the content defined as Level 5, even if they have not achieved Level 4 or are insecure with the work at that level: 'More than most, they need to consolidate new learning as well as catching up on unlearned skills' (DfEE 2001: 1/34). And hereby lies the challenge, be it one of accountability or intent. It is blatant nonsense to expect a pupil to learn Level 5 content, as well as learning Level 4, while perhaps consolidating Level 3. For experienced teachers used to returning to topics again and again to offer pupils opportunities for revising or working on the mathematics in different contexts there will be few problems. The difference will lie in the management of the curriculum to fit the Framework.

If we take the key objectives, those in Years 5 and 6 relate strongly to those in Year 7 (and in the Framework school years are directly related to the Levels in the National Curriculum). The first key objective in Year 7 relates to fractions, decimals and percentages. The related objectives in Years 5 and 6, given in Table 3.1, will no doubt be used and revisited by teachers in order to address the Year 7 key objective while providing a sound learning environment for their pupils.

Table 3.1 Some connected key objectives from Years 5, 6 and 7 curricula

Year	Key objectives
5	Multiply and divide and positive integer up to 10 000 by 10 or 100 and understand the effect
6	Multiply and divide decimals mentally by 10 or 100, integers by 1000, and explain the effect
5	Use decimal notation for tenths and hundredths
5	Round a number with one or two decimal places to the nearest integer
6	Order a mixed set of numbers with up to three decimal places
5	Relate fractions to division and their decimal representations
6	Use a fraction as an operator to find fractions of numbers or quantities
6	Understand percentage as the number of parts in every 100, and find simple percentages of small whole-number quantities
6	Solve simple problems involving ratio and proportion
7	Recognise the equivalence of percentages, fractions and decimals

The next useful thing to do is to connect the mathematics together. A list like the one above often assumes hierarchies that do not make sense for teaching. When looking at connecting mathematics we draw 'splurge' diagrams (Prestage and Perks 2001). If we begin with the Year 7 objective, much of the Years 5 and 6 content would appear as aspects of the mathematics to be considered, taught, practised, learned, consolidated and checked when teaching this topic (Figure 3.2).

The remaining key objectives can be connected in a similar way, so that it is possible to bring much of the mathematics to all pupils who will only be working at Level 5 if it is appropriate. It would be worth exploring the mathematics of these key

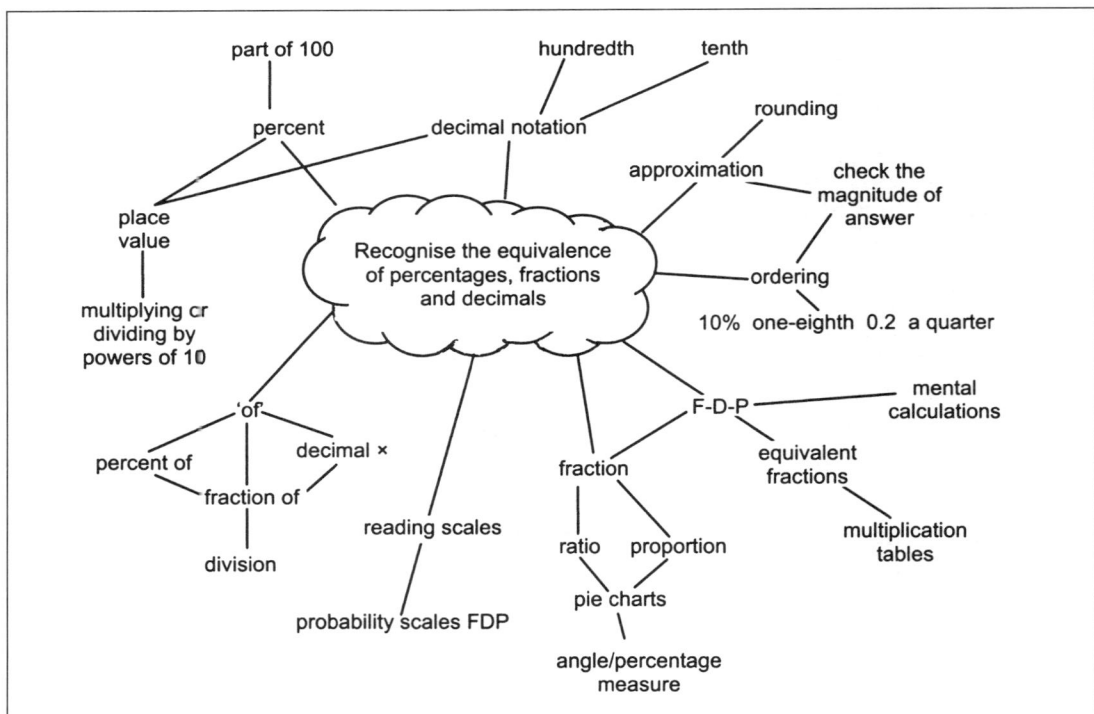

Figure 3.2 Splurge diagram connecting fractions, decimals and percentages

objectives with the rest of your department, constructing a curriculum that concentrates on these objectives; 14 in all if you integrate Ma1.

We would agree with Daniels and Anghileri in their plea for those with special educational needs, that there is a style of teaching that can help all pupils:'Teaching that is responsive to learner needs; that builds on pupil understanding; that respects individual contributions as the basis for negotiation of mathematical understandings, lies at the heart of our model for the way forward' (1995: 151).

Summary

In this chapter we have looked at the advice on direct teaching, alternative lesson styles to challenge the orthodoxy of the three-part lesson and the place of inclusion in a policy that assumes that a large majority of pupils can work with Level 5 material.

> a key factor in national attainment is the degree to which the curriculum is differentiated . . . On the whole successful countries, like those on the Pacific rim, maintain an ambitious curriculum for all pupils, whereas countries which offer some children a reduced curriculum, like Britain and the United States, do less well. However the downside of this ambitious uniform curriculum is that many pupils in Pacific rim countries feel that they are not able to keep up, and hence that they are weak at mathematics.
>
> (Brown *et al.* 1998: 369)

The Framework seeks to improve standards by the imposition of an undifferentiated curriculum. But in the TIMMS results our pupils are shown to be better able to do the mathematics in context than pupils in other countries, and confident about their abilities in the subject. Demands are constantly made that we prepare our pupils for life-long learning, prepare them to be versatile so that they can respond to changing demands of the job market in order to maintain the country's wealth. We will do the country a disservice if we destroy confidence in mathematics (there are enough people who dislike it) at a time when the demands of technology make mathematical thinking even more desirable: 'our own position celebrates active learners rather than passive pupils, constructors of knowledge rather than receivers and above all individuals who have confidence to *use their own* mathematics' (Daniels and Anghileri 1995: 151, original emphasis). This also influences our own views on teaching, that direct teaching is not delivering, but directing to allow the best conditions for learning.

4 Ma1, thinking skills and solving problems

Here we are again! Just when you thought you had GCSE investigations sorted out, the National Curriculum created an attainment target, Ma1, Using and Applying Mathematics, which over the years has itself undergone various minor transformations. The current Orders for the National Curriculum (DfEE 1999b), Curriculum 2000, have integrated Ma1 into each of the areas of the programmes of study, but it is still recognisable under the three strands of problem-solving, communication and reasoning. Now the NNS emphasises the use of 'thinking skills' and we have to reconnect the old words with the new labels.

The mathematics department is responsible for its fair share of the development of students' thinking skills, but, fortunately, the 'contribution from mathematics is drawn directly from using and applying mathematics' (DfEE 2001: 1/20). So if your department is fully fledged in its attention to Ma1 then all you need do is check the new labelling for thinking skills and then account for them via the content of the Framework. For those who continue to work on Ma1 and especially its integration into the curriculum, we will give some examples explicitly from the examples in the Framework.

Ma1 and thinking skills

First let us consider the labelling of the strands of Ma1 and thinking skills (Table 4.1). The problem-solving strand is the trickiest strand to get an overview of since you might imagine (quite correctly) that pupils are solving problems all the time in mathematics lessons. True. So this strand needs unpicking. If you look at some of the sections in the National Curriculum programme of study and in the Framework section 'Using and applying mathematics to solve problems' about problem-solving in Ma1 they show a move to pupils working on problems more independently over time and then accounting to others for their decisions and solutions. Thinking about this strand in terms of making and monitoring decisions enables it to be planned for in many, if not all, of your mathematics lessons. Because of the many uses and overuse of the term 'problem-solving', which Ma1 has as its first strand, we would like to replace this phrase with the label from the previous National Curriculum orders (Department of Education and Science (DES)/Welsh Office (WO) 1991), 'making and monitoring choices', as this is easier to plan for in a classroom. It is also easier to see that pupils are developing in their decision-making. So instead of problem-solving, the label that we will use for the rest of this chapter for the first strand of Ma1 is 'making and monitoring choices'.

Table 4.1 Ma1 and thinking skills

Ma1	Thinking skills
Problem solving Communicating Reasoning	Information processing skills Enquiry skills Creative thinking skills Reasoning skills Evaluation skills

Section 1, pages 20–22, of the Framework (DfEE 2001) offers clear connections relating the requirements of the National Curriculum for Ma1 and definitions of thinking skills. The Framework is explicit about the relationships between these. You will be expected to account for thinking skills. The first key responsibility of the head of department is 'to *lead an audit* of the standards, planning, teaching and assessment of mathematics at Key Stage 3, using the criteria in the Framework' (DfEE 2001: 1/7, original emphasis). In terms of auditing your curriculum, carry on working with Ma1, know how Ma1 is integrated into your curriculum but also know how the thinking skills programme is addressed in that curriculum. It might also be an opportunity for the whole department to think again about Ma1 and so we start with an overview of each of these three strands. The National Curriculum Council (NCC) (1992a,b) documents have a very helpful analysis of Ma1, summarised here.

- *Making and monitoring choices* is about pupils making decisions about problems and methods and monitoring their decision-making. It includes pupils selecting the mathematics, materials and resources to use, planning methods, checking the information and reviewing progress.
- The *mathematical communication* strand is about pupils formulating, discussing, interpreting data, recording and presenting findings for a variety of purposes in a variety of ways. Mathematical communication arises out of different purposes, including expressing your own ideas, making sense of what others say and write, and clarifying your own ideas.
- The *reasoning strand* is about pupils finding solutions and giving justification. It involves pupils of all ages developing the ideas of generalisation, argument and proof. Finding solutions includes aiming for a generalisation or a conclusion. Giving justifications includes convincing yourself and others that your solutions are correct. The reasoning strand should be thought of in terms of the breadth of possibilities of finding solution and giving justifications, from 'most pupils in our class walk to school', to 'the interior angles in a triangle add to 180 degrees', to '√2 is an irrational number'.

You might like to think about some mathematics that you have done recently or some mathematics that you have observed pupils doing. While you are recalling the task, try to identify some of the decisions that were made or decisions that the task set required the solver to make. How did you communicate your ideas or justify your solution?

Any mathematics that you plan can include some aspect of Ma1. One route into this is to consider the choices that the pupils are being asked to make in any task that you set. If the pupils are allowed to make choices and are then expected to monitor and justify those choices they will be working on aspects of Ma1. However, it is for the teacher to make the decision about the extent to which the pupils are to be offered choices. Depending on the focus for the lesson the teacher can decide to extend or limit the choices. In this way Ma1 can begin to permeate the other aspects of the mathematics curriculum described in Ma2–4.

Here are two mathematics questions that we came across recently. The questions are taken from different Year 7 mathematics curricula for the pupils to work on over a period of time (so much for the tightly controlled, 60-minute, three-part lesson). Monitor what you are doing and see how it matches the three strands in Ma1.

> How many isosceles triangles can be found if the areas must be 9cm² and all three vertices lie on a grid point, one of which must be (3, 1)?

> Jack and Jill have each been given a share a piece of land within a rectangle. Move the boundary line between the two parts so that it is perpendicular to the outer boundaries and so that the share of land is the same.
>
>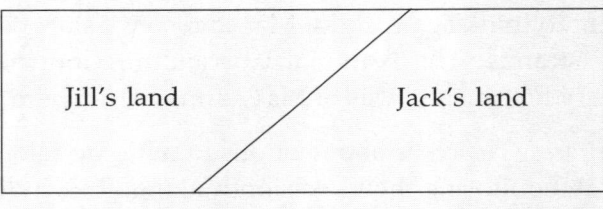

We will next take each of the headings and explanations from the thinking skills strand and show how we would match them, although in many of the strands the matching is fairly obvious. You may then like to return to these problems and see if you can identify the thinking skills involved.

Information-processing skills

> These enable pupils to find and organise relevant information, to compare and contrast it, and to identify and analyse relationships.
>
> (DfEE 2001: 1/20)

This thinking skill belongs mainly to the communication strand, although it also includes some aspects of making and monitoring decision as the pupils decide what data to collect and how collect them, and some aspects of reasoning as the pupils begin to analyse the data they have collected.

One of the examples given suggests that pupils are using information-processing skills when they 'process the information in a 2D picture of a 3D object'. One of the difficulties with such a statement is that unless the pupils do something with the information, you are in no position to judge the quality of the information-processing. For assessment purposes this may not be a useful label.

Enquiry skills

Enquiry skills enable pupils to ask questions, define questions for enquiry, plan, research, predict outcomes, anticipate consequences and draw conclusions.

(DfEE 2001: 1/21)

This encompasses a mixture of the complete flow of Ma1, with:

- asking questions and defining questions as part of the making and monitoring choices strand;
- representing problems and solutions as part of the communication strand;
- predicting and justifying outcomes as part of the reasoning strand.

Examples given suggest that enquiry skills are developed when pupils:

modify a problem they have solved to create a new problem: for example, when they find the smallest number with exactly three factors, then extend this to four factors, or other numbers of factors. They use enquiry skills when they find and eliminate alternatives.

(1/21)

The language of the examples adds yet more possibilities to the collection of processes within Ma1.

Creative thinking skills

These enable pupils to generate and develop ideas, to hypothesise, to apply imagination and to seek innovative alternatives.

(DfEE 2001: 1/21)

This category belongs to the reasoning strand. Generating and developing ideas and suggesting hypotheses are familiar mathematical processes and 'innovative alternatives' could be interesting, but are probably unacceptable in SATs, but we remain curious about how we might teach someone to 'apply imagination'.

Reasoning skills

These enable pupils to give reasons for opinions and actions, to infer and deduce, to make informed judgements and decisions and to use precise language to reason.

(DfEE 2001: 1/22)

This category also belongs to the reasoning strand and we leave it to departments to discover the difference between this and creative reasoning skills when it comes to suggesting hypotheses and drawing inferences.

Evaluation skills

These enable pupils to develop and apply evaluation criteria and to judge the value of information and ideas.

(DfEE 2001: 1/22)

This skill belongs mainly in the monitoring strand of 'making and monitoring choices', although there are also some elements of reasoning in the definition given.

All of these terms (and many others) are useful ways of describing how pupils may be working when they are doing mathematics. The three strands of Ma1 offer an overview of the processes, but there are times when you will want different levels of detail.

The place of problems in the Framework

You and your departmental colleagues will have worked on what you think Ma1 is, and you may, like us, reject 'problem-solving' because it is a not useful category for thinking about Ma1. One of the major reasons for this is the many ways in which problem-solving is interpreted. In mathematics textbooks, problems often seem to be mathematics expressed in words. Before the introduction of investigational work, most experiences of problems were based on the peculiar questions specific to mathematics classrooms. We practised questions written in numbers only, followed by 'problems' where the same mathematical operations had to be deduced from the words. In the USA they go even further. You can get problems categorised into one-stage, two-stage and more-stage problems (Table 4.2).

Table 4.2 Staged problems

One-stage	Jo has five sweets, and Ben has seven. How many more sweets does Ben have than Jo?
Two-stage	Jo has $7 and Ben has $5. If they club together to buy a kite costing $10.50, how much money will they have left?

One-stage problems need only one mathematical operation; two-stage problems need two. We have all seen these types of problems and we will continue seeing them in tests, examinations and worksheets. They are problems for many pupils, because extracting the information and choosing the correct operations takes skill. Often, however, in these problems, there is little opportunity for Ma1 and few opportunities for pupils to demonstrate their thinking skills.

The Framework declares that:

> A problem can serve as an introduction, to assess pupils' prior knowledge or to set a context for the work; it can be used to provide motivation for acquiring a skill; or it can be set as a class activity or as homework towards the end of a topic so that pupils use and apply the mathematics they have been taught.   (DfEE 2001: 1/20)

Wonderful! A problem can be used at any stage in any lesson for any purpose: the choice belongs to the teacher. There are no surprises there: that's what we do in mathematics lessons.

For each of Years 7 to 9, the Framework includes a section of bulleted objectives called 'using and applying mathematics to solve problems', with exemplar assessment items. In this section we look at the definition and progression and expected outcomes in the Framework for 'using and applying mathematics to solve problems'. The Framework appears to offer an alternative to the descriptors in the statutory Ma1, and you need to know how to match these differences.

The objectives

Table 4.3 shows the objectives for the area of 'applying mathematics and solving problems'. The bold type represents key objectives. There is a shift in objectives over the three school years (see the emphasis in the key objectives shown by bold type).

Table 4.3 Objectives for applying mathematics and solving problems

Example pages	Year 7	Year 8	Year 9
2–35	Applying mathematics and solving problems		
2–25	**Solve word problems and investigate in a range of contexts**	Solve more demanding problems and investigate in a range of contexts	Solve increasingly demanding problems and evaluate solutions; explore connections in mathematics across a range of contexts
26–7	Identify the necessary information to solve a problem	**Identify the necessary information to solve a problem; represent problems and interpret solutions in algebraic, geometric or graphical form**	Represent problems and synthesise infromation (in various forms); move from one form to another to gain a different perspective on a problem
28–9	**Break a complex calculation into simpler steps, choosing and using appropriate and efficient operations and methods** and resources including ICT	Solve more complex problems by breaking them into smaller steps or tasks	**Solve substantial problems by breaking them into simpler tasks, using a range of techniques, methods and resources including ICT**
30–31	Present and interpret solutions, justifying inferences and explaining solutions; **explain and justify methods and conclusions**	**Use logical argument to establish the truth of a statement**	**Present a precise, reasoned argument, making use of symbols, diagrams and graphs and related explanatory text**
32–5	Suggest extensions, begin to generalise and to understand the significance of counter-example	Suggest extensions, conjecture and generalise; identify exceptional cases or counter-examples	Suggest extensions to problems; conjecture and generalise; identify exceptional cases or counter-examples, explaining why

Table 4.4 Objectives for problem solving given in Section 4

Example pages	Year 7	Year 8	Year 9
2–35	Applying mathematics and solving problems		
2–25	**Solve word problems and investigate in a range of contexts**		
2–9	• problems involving money, percentages, ratio and proportion, number and algebra		
10–13	• problems to solve with a graphical calculator		
14–21	• problems involving shape, space and measures		
22–5	• problems involving handling data		
26–7	**Identify the necessary information to solve a problem; represent problems mathematically in a variety of forms**		
28	**Break problems into smaller steps and tasks; choose and use efficient operations, methods and resources**		
30	**Present and interpret solutions, explaining and justifying methods, inferences and reasoning**		
32–5	**Suggest extension, conjecture; identify exceptional cases or counter-examples**		

The language of proof is significantly missing, which is an area of concern to the mathematical community. The closest we get is the 'significance of counter-example'.

So you have to return to the three strands of Ma1 to plan, in your teaching, for pupils to 'solve problems'. It may be true that if you are solving a problem then you would be by default engaged in problem-solving strategies, even in the one-stage problem in Table 4.2. But the opportunities for any strategy may be very limited. Also, pupils may be solving problems where these strategies are neither overt nor obvious. Problems have to be chosen where such strategies have to be demonstrated. There is little in the text of the Framework that defines strategies better than the National Curriculum, and it is interesting that the Framework itself returns to the National Curriculum for its explanation of thinking skills. All of these objectives are within the National Curriculum and within the definitions of Ma1, so, as was mentioned earlier, if your department is covering Ma1 satisfactorily at the moment then you also will be covering this section.

Using the examples to exploit Ma1

In Section 4 there are 33 pages of exemplar material for this strand, with 23 of these devoted to 'solving problems' of increasing complexity. But what are the problems defined in this section? What are they to be used for? In fact, these examples seem to herald a move away from Ma1 and a return to traditional definitions of problems. You have to use the suggestions wisely, as they are often not rich in Ma1 processes. They do, however, provide suggestions of 'tricky' problems that will be found at the end of Key Stage tests. (There would not be time in a timed written test for a fully fledged Ma1 question.)

There is an array of word problems that you could easily adapt and use within the topic area. As we suggested above, you could use these at any stage in a topic. You can find problems in the examples that can be easily tweaked to create opportunities for Ma1. Some are very much assessment items, examples to be covered in a limited time, and yet others can be redefined to exploit Ma1. All of the following examples are taken from Section 4.

Examples to use for teaching topics

Year 7: Sequences

> Here is a sequence of five numbers:
>
> 2 □ □ □ 18
>
> The rule is to start with 2 then add the same amount each time. Write in the missing numbers. (DfEE 2001: 4/8)

Year 8: Angles

> A diagram shows two overlapping squares and a straight line. The pupil is asked to calculate the missing angles from the diagram. (DfEE 2001: 4/17)

Year 9: Probability

> Two bags, A and B, contain coloured cubes. Each has the same number of cubes in it. The probability of taking a red cube at random out of bag A is 0.5, and out of B it is 0.2. All the cubes are put into an empty new bag. What is the probability of taking a red cube out of the new bag?
>
> (DfEE 2001: 4/23)

Examples that can be tweaked for Ma1

Ma1 emerges in classrooms when pupils generate several examples and begin to look for patterns, to make hypotheses and justify them. Often it is a case of producing more examples from which to make and test an hypothesis.

Year 7

> More problems to solve with a graphical calculator:
>
> Draw the line joining (3, 1) to (6, 1).
>
> Draw a parallelogram standing on this line.
>
> Now draw a hexagon standing on this line.
>
> Draw another shape standing on the line.
>
> What if the starting points are (3, 1) and (4, 5)? (DfEE 2001: 4/12)

The example offers an interesting starting point, but there is still little opportunity for pupils to specialise in order to generalise. An interesting generalisation lies in the relationship of the coordinates of the vertices.

> - Draw several parallelograms.
> - Two of the vertices are (3, 1) and (6, 1). Record the other vertices of the different parallelograms. What relationships can you find?

This task may not be sufficiently challenging for some pupils because one side of the parallelogram is parallel to an axis. This is easily made more challenging by changing the points to (3, 1) and (6, 0), or even (3, 1) and (–2, –1). This is the sort of change that anyone who is testing hypotheses is likely to make, before they go to the algebra of, say, the points (a, b) and (c, d).

The example could be done using pencil and paper, a spreadsheet or a graphical package as well as a graphical calculator, and the resources may change the emphasis of the mathematics.

Year 8

Triangles are made by joining three of the vertices of a cube. How many different shapes can the triangles have? How many shapes are isosceles triangles? How many are equilateral triangles? Which of the triangles has the largest area? Justify your answer.   (DfEE 2001: 4/33)

- Remove the closed questions and ask the pupils to sort and classify the different triangles and describe their properties.

Year 9

Find the smallest number greater than 50 that has the same number of factors as 50. Justify your answer.   (DfEE 2001: 4/7)

- What other numbers have the same number of factors as 50?
- Can you predict which they will be before you find them?

If a number is expressed as a product of its prime factors it is possible to state the number of factors the number has.

Examples that you could develop to get some Ma1

The same sorts of developments are needed as in the examples in the previous section, but you need to take a bit of a leap away from the type of questions you meet in tests; take time to develop that creativity and 'to apply imagination and to look for innovative outcomes' (DfEE 2001: 1/18).

Year 7

There are 3 chocolate biscuits in every 5 biscuits in a box. There are 30 biscuits altogether in the box. How many of them are chocolate biscuits?   (DfEE 2001: 4/4)

- What is the ratio of chocolate biscuits to non-chocolate biscuits?
- What happens to this ratio as you begin to eat the biscuits?
- What different ratios are possible? Why?
- What other ratios could you have started with?

Year 8

The chocolate bars in a full box weighed 2kg in total. Each bar was the same size. Eight of the bars were eaten. The bars left in the box weighed 1.5kg altogether. How many chocolate bars were in the original box?   (DfEE 2001: 4/5)

- What if the chocolate bars were biscuits and were not all the same size?
- What if the chocolate bars were carrots and were not all the same size? How many different solutions might you get?
- How many samples of 8 carrots would you need to be 'certain' of your estimate?

Year 9

> Two isosceles triangles have the same base AD. Angle ACD is twice the size of angle
> ABD. Call these angles $2x$ and x. Prove that angle a is always half of angle x.
>
> (DfEE 2001: 4/17)

> • Ask the pupils to show that angle ACD is twice the size of angle ABD.
>   What is triangle ABD is not isosceles?

The removal of a resource can make the task more interesting mathematically. Would this be possible to do with a graphical package or a geometry package? Would the task be easier/harder if the ratio of the areas was different?

Whether you find the examples helpful in developing in this way is a personal decision. We look for ideas everywhere and adapt them; we like to have different problems all the time. You probably have your own favourites for Ma1. However, the Framework examples are insufficient for exploiting Ma1, unless they are adapted. You may prefer to leave them as assessment practice.

Summary

Solving problems is one of the areas in which English pupils did well in TIMMS (Brown *et al.* 1998). It is worth us thinking about maintaining the enthusiasm that is found in the earlier years of secondary school to develop mathematical creativity. Changing problems to increase pupil choice is, for us, one of the most important aspects of mathematics teaching (Prestage and Perks 2001). Working on the examples in the Framework to create new Ma1 tasks strongly linked to the other mathematical content is a valuable way of working in a departmental meeting. One of the biggest issues for departments is to maintain their own and their pupils' enthusiasm for mathematics. Talking about mathematics with your peers can be very rewarding, as is working on the new problems you invent. Mathematical curiosity is very energising.

The Framework offers no real guidance for Ma1. The more recent focus on thinking skills means that we still need to consider the role of Ma1 in teaching. Ma1, unlike thinking skills, is statutory, and using the Framework does not mean that we can ignore the National Curriculum. The examples on problem-solving do not offer many ways of including Ma1 and you will need to continue with your existing implementation of the National Curriculum for this attainment target.

5 What's new in Ma2–4?

As with any new definition or interpretation of the school curriculum all departments will have to investigate differences to the content of the curriculum and then decide how to accommodate those differences. Although the Framework is based on the National Curriculum there are changes of emphasis and, in places, a different interpretation of the programme of study. Also, the major demand, already discussed in earlier chapters, that the majority of Year 7 pupils be taught Level 5 material from the National Curriculum will require most comprehensive school departments to make an audit of the Year 7 syllabus and be confident about changes that might be necessary.

In this chapter we highlight the differences between the presentation of the curriculum in the National Curriculum and in the Framework.

Ma2: Number and Algebra

In the 'Number' and 'Algebra' strands the differences between the National Curriculum and the Framework vary in size. There are no differences for the first section, 'Number and the number system', other than a change in headings. The five headings in the National Curriculum were 'Integers', 'Powers and Roots', 'Fractions', 'Decimals' and 'Percentages and Ratio', whereas the Framework groups the same material into three groups, 'Place Value, Ordering and Rounding', 'Integers, Powers and Roots' and 'Fractions, Decimals, Percentages, Ratio and Proportion'. This is a cosmetic change only. (For reference, see Tables 2.8–2.10, showing the summary objectives from Section 4 and the headings.) There is much the same content in this section but it is grouped slightly differently.

You will need to look carefully at the Framework section headed 'Calculations', as it contains the main thrust of the NNS with objectives for mental methods, written methods and calculator methods. In fact there are few differences in content from the National Curriculum but there is a definite change in emphasis. There is the addition of 'rapid recall of number facts' to the 'Mental Methods' section and the removal of the whole section 'Solving Numerical Problems ' (presumably because this is classed by the Framework as belonging to Ma1). There is a new section, 'Checking Results', in which the words from the National Curriculum (DfEE 1999: 46) become a key objective for the Framework: 'consider whether a result is of the right order of magnitude' (DfEE 2001: 3/6).

It is worth pausing here for a few moments to consider methods of calculation. The primary NNS has a strong focus on the use of mental methods and written methods and this has been carried through to the KS3 Framework. The role of mental methods, and the appropriateness of written methods, need discussion in the age of the calculator. Despite the Framework's focus on ICT, the role of the calculator is still not fully addressed and, as with GCSE and non-calculator papers, there still seems to be a failure to recognise the ways in which calculators can be used sensibly to work with number.

Mental methods

> An ability to calculate mentally lies at the heart of numeracy.   (DfEE 2001: 1/10)

The KS3 Framework stresses the need for continuity of emphasis on mental methods from KS2. The pupils are expected to:

- remember number facts and recall them without hesitation;
- use facts that are known to figure out new facts; for example, knowing that half of 250 is 125 can be used to work out 250 – 123;
- draw on a repertoire of mental strategies to work out calculations like 326 – 81, 223 × 4 or 2.5% of £3000, with some thinking time;
- understand and use the relationships between operations to work out answers and check results.

Recalling number facts has always been the standard by which most people judge numeracy. (What is 7 × 8?) The multiplication tables still have to be learned, but what other facts are needed? Pupils need a repertoire. Does this mean that they should have party tricks: multiplying by 9 on your fingers; multiplying two figure numbers by 11, doubling and doubling and doubling? These are all fine, as long as they are not just feats of memory. Doubling makes the two times table easy, and the four times table and the eight times table, etc. but only if pupils connect doubling with the two times table, and link this to other aspects of multiplication, such as the type of extension shown in Figure 5.1. Doubling also needs to be connected with halving and dividing by two. We also need to know why we are asking pupils to do this work. It should not be just to pass mental arithmetic tests. Mental methods need a purpose.

Written methods

Care needs to be taken with the transition from mental to written methods. Despite the focus on these transitions, these do not always follow tidily, as the Framework suggests: 'The progression towards written methods is crucial, since standard written methods are based on steps which are done mentally and which need to be secured first' (DfEE 2000b: 3/10). Research shows that there is sometimes a mismatch between mental methods and standard written ones: 'written versions of children's mental strategies show little similarity to standard algorithms and . . . are based on a different understanding of number' (Anghileri 2000: 136). The standard long multiplication algorithm bears little relationship to mental methods (have a look at this and check it for yourself). You may want to choose a mental method that links to

```
27 × 18 =

                                              27 × 1 = 27
              18 = 16 + 2 so                  27 × 2 = 54
  so     27 × 18 = 27 × (16 + 2)              27 × 4 = 108
                 = 27 × 16 + 27 × 2           27 × 8 = 216
                 = 432 + 54                   27 × 16 = 432
                 = 486

          27 × 18 = 486
```

Figure 5.1 Multiplication by doubling

a different written method, which you may prefer for your pupils. For example, a method favoured in Holland (Anghileri 2000) for two figure multiplication links doubling with a written method (Figure 5.1). The method is also easily extended to division using repeated subtraction.

The Framework suggests a single standard algorithm for multiplication; the one shown on the left in Figure 5.2. Knowledge of this, the Framework also suggests, shows progress from the 'grid' method, which is said to be an informal method (DfEE 2000b: 1/10). We have to admit to not understanding the difference. Both are algorithms; both are efficient; both always work. We do not know why one is preferred.

Another issue arising from a focus on a single standard written method is that it is not always the most efficient. The most general method – i.e. the one which always works because it works in all cases – is advocated, so when do we introduce other methods, which may be more efficient for some calculations? For example, multiplying a three-digit number by 25 is more easily done by dividing it by 4 and then multiplying by 100, than using the long multiplication method (Figure 5.2). How will pupils choose?

There is also the issue of why we are teaching written methods, when in the outside world the calculator will be used. Boaler reminds us that neither professional mathematicians nor professional users 'spend their time reproducing standard procedures – that is, a peculiar practice specific to the mathematics classroom. Yet the specificity of that practice may be the single most important factor reducing achievement and affiliation for students' (2000: 380). But at this point in time the calculator argument has not been won.

```
        673
      ×  25
      _____
      13460                      673 ÷ 4 = 168.25
       3365                  168.25 × 100 = 16825
      _____
      16825
```

Figure 5.2 Two methods of calculation

Using a calculator

The Framework shows clear guidance in the exemplar material (Section 4) on the importance of graphical calculators to work on mathematics, but offers little in the way of encouraging use of their less distinguished counterparts (DfEE 2001: 1/12). As a calculating tool the calculator is not preferred.

> Before Year 5, the calculator's main role in mathematics is not as a calculating tool, since pupils are still developing the mental calculation skills and written methods that they will need in later years. But it does offer a unique way of learning about mathematical ideas, throughout all Key Stages. (DfEE 2001: 1/12)

Learning to use calculators is useful; they are around in the outside world. Pupils need to learn how to use them sensibly: to check for sensible answers, to estimate, and to know which operation to use. Using calculators does not stop you from doing mathematics, rather it can enhance mathematical understanding as children have the independence to explore structure and look for the underlying mathematical ideas (Ruthven 2000). However, poor use can lead to bad habits and reliance in situations when more thought is required. We need to work on 'Limited, strictly controlled, but effective use of calculators' (Burghes 1999: 145). These words can seem very restrictive, but one of the problems we can have when pupils come to the use of calculators after they have failed with arithmetic is their assumption that calculators will always 'do it better'. As teachers we need to see control not as stopping their use but as using the power of the calculator for exploring mathematics.

Calculator use needs to be limited on some occasions, but you have to decide when to use them, and when to limit their use. For example, if pupils are practising chanting the seven times table, a calculator would halt the purpose of the activity. But if pupils are exploring the patterns in the units digits of the seven times table a calculator creates accurate results for exploration. Pupils might compare 49×7 with 9×7 and 119×7 to develop a checking strategy about the last digit in an integer product.

When pupils are playing a game such as Four in a Row (see Figure 5.3), the calculator has an important role once decisions about which numbers to use have been

30	7	90	275	15	63
390	225	165	23	27	195
375	161	21	75	39	13
99	33	69	3	690	77
25	175	11	92	330	135
117	299	450	45	325	750

Four in a Row: multiplication

A game for two players.

You need a calculator, and each player needs a set of counters.

Take turns to play the game. Choose two numbers from the box below and multiply them together on the calculator. If the number is on the grid (and free), claim it by covering it with a counter. The first to get a line of four counters in any direction (do not forget diagonals) **wins**!

1	3	7	9	11
13	15	23	25	30

Plan ahead!

Figure 5.3 Calculator 'Four in a Row'

made. Deciding how to win a certain square depends on mental strategies. Using the calculator ensures that the calculation is correct, so the calculator is taking part as a referee.

Algebra

The two main headings in the Algebra section of the Framework remain the same as in the National Curriculum: 'Equalities, Formulae and Identities' and 'Sequences, Functions and Graphs'. The Framework does not use the subheadings of the National Curriculum, although the bullet points follow these headings.

You may not introduce algebra to your Year 7 pupils until you feel that they are ready, so this may be an area that you need to check. We will explore the treatment of the following section from the National Curriculum on 'Using Symbols' and see how the Framework interprets it for the yearly programmes.

> Distinguish the different roles played by letter symbols in algebra, knowing that letter symbols represent definite unknown numbers in equations [for example, $5x + 1 = 16$], defined quantities of variables in formulae [for example, $V = IR$], general, unspecified and independent numbers in identities [for example, $3x + 2x = 5x$, $(x + 1)^2 = x^2 + 2x + 1$ for all values of x] and in functions they define new expressions or quantities by referring to known quantities [for example, $y = 2x$]. (DfEE 1999: 47)

The interpretation in the Framework is shown in Table 5.1.

Taken as a whole there is no real difference, but if you look at each of the years separately (and separation is a feature of the Framework) you may want to question why Year 7 pupils have to deal with the words 'term', 'expression' and 'equation', but not 'formula', when they will already have met formulae for perimeter and area of rectangles in primary school. You may want to question how the Year 9 objective is different from the Year 8 objective. And having questioned these things you may choose to carry on with what you normally do. Over KS3, with external assessment in Year 9, you can work in the way suggested by the National Curriculum: only the introduction of Year 7 and Year 8 reported SATs might change this decision.

As we have reported elsewhere, the objective written with the examples is in its most succinct form. There are examples in the Framework to illustrate the meaning of the teaching objective (DfEE 2001: 4/112), which show a progression from Year 7 to Year 9. The layers of the National Curriculum definition across Years 7–9 given in Table 5.1 may be of value, but for most teachers the shorter objective on page 112 of the Framework is likely to be the most memorable and useful.

Table 5.1 Framework interpretation of 'Using Symbols' in the National Curriculum

Year 7 (p. 6)	**Use letters and symbols to represent unknown numbers or variables**; know the meanings of the words *term*, *expression* and *equation*.
Year 8 (p. 8)	Begin to distinguish the different roles played by letter symbols in equations, formulae and functions; know the meaning of the words *formula* and *function*.
Year 9 (p. 10)	Distinguish the different roles played by letter symbols in equations, identities, formulae and functions.
Examples (p. 112)	Use letters and symbols and distinguish their different roles in algebra.

The next difference that we found was one of interpretation. We assumed that most of the key objectives would match the Level 5 descriptors. However, that is not the case. A teaching objective for Year 7 in the Framework is the following key objective:

> **Generate co-ordinate pairs that satisfy a simple linear rule; plot the graphs of simple linear functions** (DfEE 2001: 3/6)

In fact the National Curriculum only states that at Level 5 pupils should 'use and interpret coordinates in all four quadrants'. Building on this, the teaching objective for Year 8 is:

> **Generate points in all four quadrants and plot the graphs of linear functions where** y **is given explicitly in terms of** x, on paper and using ICT; **recognise that equations in the form** $y = mx + c$ **correspond to straight-line graphs.** (DfEE 2001: 3/8)

And for Year 9:

> Generate points and plot graphs of linear functions (y is given implicitly in terms of x) e.g. $ay + bx = 0$, $y + bx + c = 0$, on paper and using ICT; **given values for** m **and** c, **find the gradient of lines given by equations of the form** $y = mx + c$. (DfEE 2001: 3/10)

None of these points of content are described explicitly in the relevant level descriptors of the National Curriculum. However, we do suspect that most departments will be working on equations of straight lines across the Key Stage and be expecting them to be tested in the higher level SATs.

Another difference that we pick up on here, but that in fact threads through much of the document, is the emphasis on real-life situations. This is evident in the National Curriculum but is much more explicit in the Framework. For examples, see Table 5.2.

Table 5.2   The Framework and real-life graphs

Year 7 (p. 6)	Begin to plot and interpret the graphs of simple linear function arising from real-life situations.
Year 8 (p. 8)	Construct linear functions arising from real-life problems and plot their corresponding graphs; discuss and interpret graphs arising from real situations.
Year 9 (p. 10)	**Construct functions arising from real-life problems and plot their corresponding graphs; interpret graphs arising from real situations**, including distance–time graphs.
Examples (p. 172)	Construct functions from real-life problems and plot and interpret their corresponding graphs.

Use of ICT means that work on practical sequences, matchstick patterns, etc., can be represented easily on a spreadsheet, leading to more manageable context based tasks. Data can be downloaded from the web to explore, and links can be made to handling data.

Ma3: 'Shape, space and measures'

This is the attainment target where the differences between the Framework and the National Curriculum are most obvious and the one for which departments will have to introduce different approaches to geometry. Our analysis offered three types of changes from the KS3 programme of study and the Levels in the Level descriptors:

- some of the teaching objectives in the Framework give an interpretation that offers more detail than we might have thought to work on;
- other objectives (especially in Year 7) are from a higher level than expected by the Framework if Year 7 is considered equivalent to Level 5, Years 8–9 to Levels 5 and 6, and Year 9 extension to Levels 7 and 8;
- some objectives offer an expansion of content from earlier versions of the National Curriculum, particularly in the areas of Euclidian geometry, proof and construction.

We will highlight the differences from and the augmentation of the curriculum using these three categories in order to help with your planning (Tables 5.3–5.5), although we ask for forbearance as the Framework still presents a measure of ambiguity.

Table 5.3 Year 7 – analysis of changes from the National Curriculum (p. 3/7)

1	Understand and use the language and notation associated with reflections, translations and rotations. Recognise and visualise the transformation and symmetry of a 2D shape. Find coordinates of points determined by geometric information. Measure and draw lines to the nearest millimetre. Read and interpret scales on a range of measuring instruments. Calculate the perimeter and area of shapes made from rectangles.
2	Using step-by-step deductions and explaining with diagrams and text (related to angle, side and symmetry properties of triangles and quadrilaterals). Use 2D representations to visualise 3D shapes and deduce some of their properties. Calculate the surface area of cubes and cuboids.
3	Construct a triangle given two sides and the included angle (SAS) or two angles and the included side (ASA). Use a ruler and protractor to construct simple nets of 3D shapes, e.g. cuboid, regular tetrahedron, square-based pyramid, triangular prism.

Table 5.4 Year 8 – analysis of changes from the National Curriculum (p. 3/9)

1	Make simple scale drawings. Given the coordinates of the points A and B, find the mid-point of the line segment AB.
2	Calculate volumes and surface areas of compound shapes made from cuboids. Know that if two 2-D shapes are congruent, corresponding sides and angles are equal.
3	Identify alternate angles and corresponding angles; understand a proof that: • the sum of the angles of a triangle is 180° and of a quadrilateral is 360°; • the exterior angle of a triangle to the sum of the two interior angles. Construct a triangle, given three sides (SSS). Use ICT to explore these constructions. Know and use geometric properties of cuboids and shapes made from cuboids; begin to use plans and elevations. Use straight edge and compasses to construct: • the mid-point and perpendicular bisector of a line segment; • the bisector of an angle; • the perpendicular from a point to a line; • the perpendicular from a point on a line.

Table 5.5 Year 9 – analysis of changes from the National Curriculum (p. 3/11)

1	Identify reflection symmetry in 3D shapes. Use and interpret maps and scale drawings.
2	Understand congruence; *apply the conditions SSS, SAS, ASA or RHS to establish the congruence of two triangles.*
3	Solve problems using properties of angles of parallel and intersecting lines, of triangles and polygons, justifying inferences and explaining reasoning with diagrams and text. *Know that if two 2-D shapes are similar, corresponding angles are equal and corresponding sides are in the same ratio.* Know the definition of a circle and the names of its parts; explain why inscribed regular polygons can be constructed by equal divisions of a circle; *know that the tangent at any point on a circle is perpendicular to the radius at that point; explain why the perpendicular from the centre to the chord bisects the chord.* Know that translations, rotations and reflections preserve length and angle and map objects onto congruent images. Recognise that enlargements preserve angle but not length and understand the implications of enlargement for perimeter, *area and volume.* Use a straight edge and compasses to construct a triangle, given right angle, hypotenuse and side (RHS). Use ICT to explore constructions of triangles and other 2D shapes.

Italics refer to Year 9 able pupils.

In each of Tables 5.3–5.5, Section 3 highlights the major shift in the curriculum from the last version of the National Curriculum to the Framework. There have been some in the mathematics community who have wanted a return to Euclidian proof, so the symbolism has returned. The notation of SSS and SAS takes some of us back to our early days of teaching – struggling with Euclidian proofs – where we were rescued by transformational geometry. The geometry now seemed more understandable: reflection preserved shape and hence congruence. Now we have to work with both Euclidian and transformational geometry. Loci and constructions have also been given greater emphasis in the Framework.

To cope with this different emphasis in geometry, to make it manageable for the learner (and the teacher), we have had a go at connecting some of the ideas (as we began to do in Chapter 2). For example, we take the isosceles triangle as a starting point and analyse the different aspects of geometry that might emerge. Textbooks do not always connect symmetry explicitly with transformations. The idea of a mirror line as the perpendicular bisector of the line segment between object and image is rarely stressed. Yet the isosceles triangle has:

- a line of symmetry, which is an angle bisector and perpendicular bisector;
- a line of symmetry, which divides the shape into two congruent right-angled triangles;
- equal sides, so to construct the shape we would use arcs, the locus of points a set distance from fixed distance, etc.

These properties are illustrated by Figure 5.4. There begins to be a sense of how the language and concepts are linked. We are not recommending this as a diagram to be given to pupils, but as something for you to connect the language and ideas. There are many more statements that could be made about the triangle.

Figure 5.5 shows some of the mathematical links that can be made by thinking about the mathematics of the isosceles triangle. You can no doubt add to the diagram.

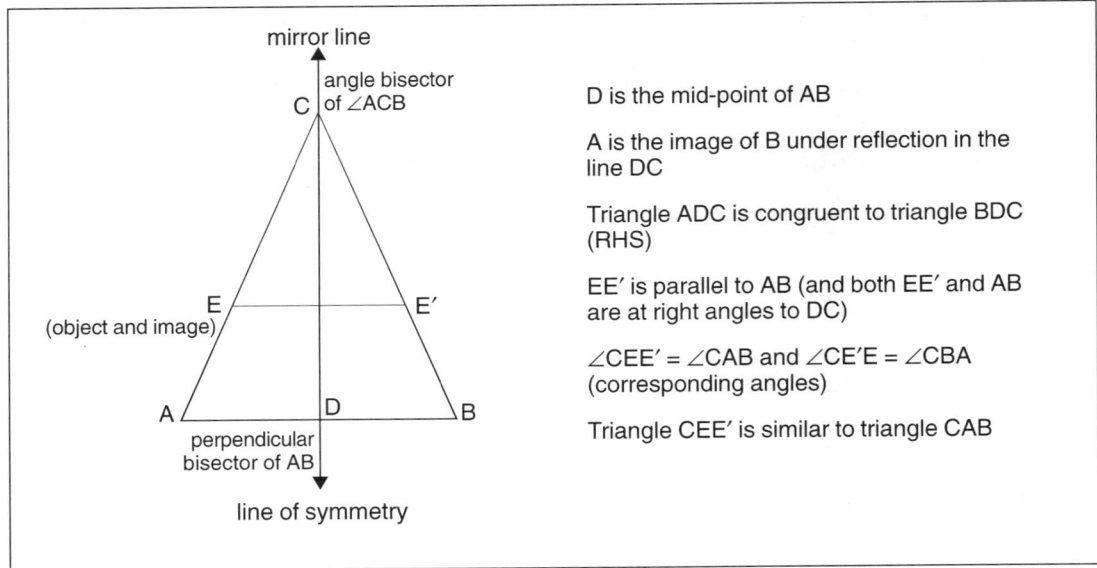

Figure 5.4   Properties of an isosceles triangle

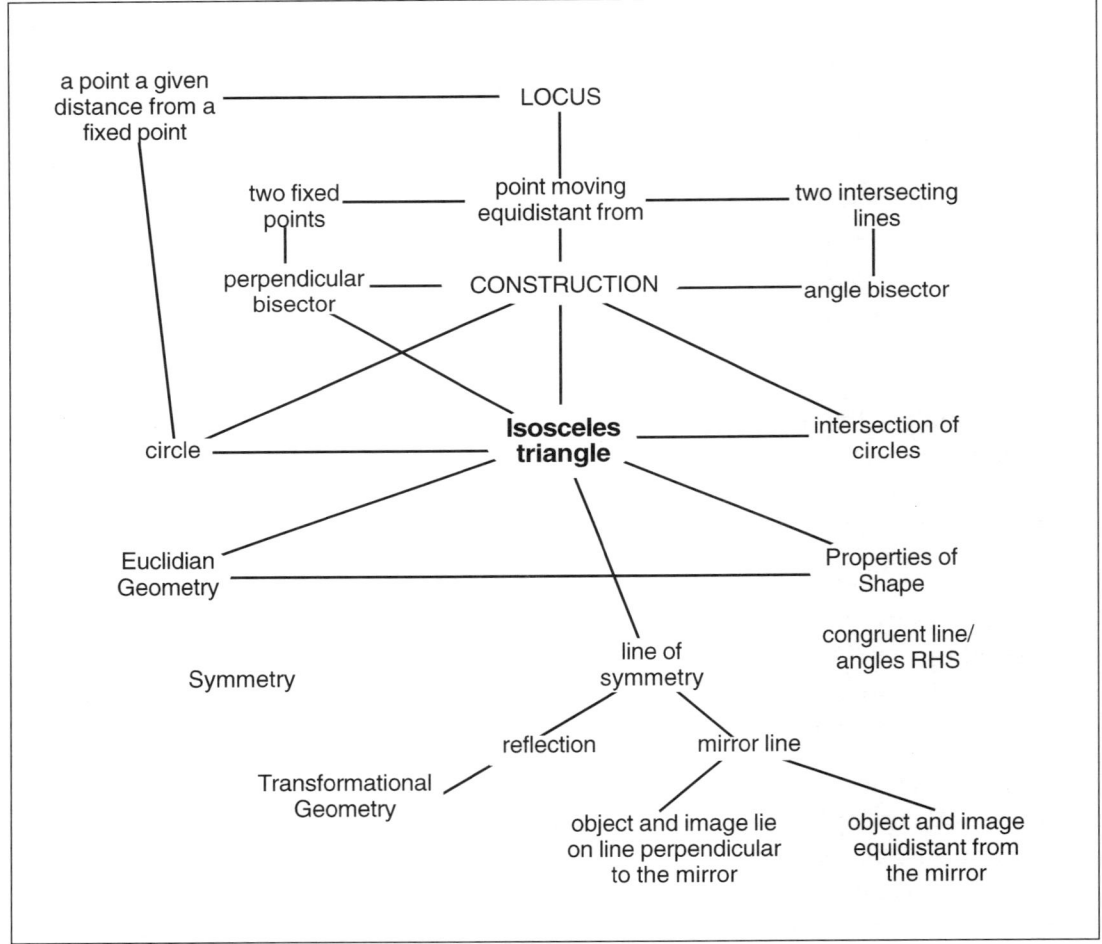

Figure 5.5   Connecting geometry via the isosceles triangle

Considered in this way, the geometry becomes more manageable. We have found it useful in our own mathematical thinking to work, for example, on understanding locus and construction as the same mathematics.

Finally for this section, there is a welcome emphasis on the use of ICT for geometry. The use of a dynamic geometry package can help to add to pupils' understanding. We hope you enjoy this approach to geometry (see Chapter 6 for some examples).

Ma4: 'Handling data'

The content in this area remains much the same, but there is much greater emphasis, as you work towards the extensions in Year 9, on analysis and interpretation. Pupils are expected to develop a critical awareness of the role of the data and the style of presentation of their findings. There is an emphasis on 'appropriate diagrams' (DfEE 2001: 3/7) and pupils are asked to 'justify choice of statistical representation in written presentations' (3/11). Tables 5.6–5.8 show the changes we have identified.

Frequency tables were included at this level, but grouping has been introduced. The role of ICT has become more explicit (a pity that all pie-charts cannot be drawn using ICT –

Table 5.6   The Year 7 changes to Handling Data (3/7)

Construct frequency tables for grouped discrete data.
Construct on paper and using ICT, graphs and diagrams to represent data including: • bar-line graphs; • frequency diagrams for grouped discrete data.
Use ICT to generate pie-charts.
Write a short report of a statistical enquiry and illustrate with appropriate diagrams, graphs and charts.

other than practising using a protractor there seems little point in pupils drawing them). It is only the inclusion of ICT that gives a difference. Some graphical calculators can be connected to data-logging systems; distance–time plots can be fascinating with a

Table 5.7   The Year 8 changes to Handling Data (3/9)

Collect data using data logging.

motion sensor. The physics department will no doubt have many other uses for data-logging, so this is a good opportunity for collaboration.

There is a sense of this attainment target being made more mathematical; the role of statistics is shifting from calculating and drawing to analysing, interpreting and

Table 5.8   The Year 9 changes to Handling Data (3/11)

Analyse data to find patterns and exceptions; look for cause and effect and try to explain anomalies.
Examine critically the results of a statistical enquiry, and justify choice of statistical representation in written presentations, recognising the limitations of any assumptions and their effect on conclusions drawn.
Compare experimental and theoretical probabilities in a range of contexts; appreciate the difference between mathematical explanation and experimental evidence.

developing critical approaches to data and presentation aspects often missing in mathematical statistics in schools. However, the Framework assumes that this level of critical maturity is achievable in the 11–14 curriculum.

The examples in Section 4 show the use of population pyramids and their interpretation. For us this stresses the need to liaise with other departments, which can come to be efficient for teaching and learning in the long term. Many subjects use statistics so let's use their data for interpretation. The emphasis on choosing the right statistics can only be fulfilled by considering the purpose of the data. It is only by using real data to interpret real questions that you can choose the appropriate statistics. The statistics are intended to convince about a point of view. If you have no opinion, the statistics are irrelevant. Courses such as 'Citizenship' will surely depend on appropriate interpretation of statistics. Pupils need to be able to read materials critically and to interpret numbers without assuming they have to be correct. For too long the mathematics of statistics has been seen as separate from the purpose of statistics. We are all familiar with the statement that there are 'lies, damned lies and statistics' (attributed to Mark Twain), but the educated citizen has to be able to unpick the truth from the numbers, rather than believe the lies.

With a greater use of ICT, the role of analysis and interpretation is crucial. Teachers will probably have to sacrifice work on drawing diagrams to using ICT and interpreting results if this aspect is to be possible. It will be interesting to see what aspects gain more marks in the SATs, because, unfortunately, this can influence what is seen as the most important aspect.

Summary

In this chapter we have reviewed the interpretation by the Framework of the National Curriculum in attainment targets 2 to 4. Some of the emphases have changed; some work has even been included from a higher level than might be expected; some of the changes seem more of a reinterpretation. The major change is the inclusion of more Euclidian geometry.

Apart from the Euclidian geometry in Ma3, there are few real changes to the content. You will have to decide on how much you want to change your current plans. Accounting for the Framework can happen in many different ways, and you can work in ways that suit you as long as you can justify your decisions to outsiders. The major difference that comes with the Framework lies with assuming that all pupils will be working on Levels 5 and upward in Year 7. Departments will have to consider changes to their teaching plans in the light of such an undifferentiated curriculum.

6 ICT in the Framework

There is no doubt that technology should and will change the teaching and learning of mathematics. The questions are what will change, when and how? In the Framework, there are almost 300 pages of examples that provide a rich source of ideas for adapting and extending activities for the classroom. Within these examples there are many references to using ICT to learn mathematics. At last, the move into the twenty-first century has been acknowledged by a national document!

Those of you who have little access to computers will be able to use the evidence from this document to ask for more resources. Good luck. No doubt you could transform the learning of mathematics for many of your students if you had better access to the hardware (and we don't just mean for 15 minutes a day on Individualised Learning Systems).

In this chapter we gather the suggestions for using ICT from the Framework under the different software packages to show the range and type of mathematics you will be expected to know and use. Currently, the use of computers is often timetabled well in advance. A topic may not lend itself obviously to time spent using computers, but unless the use of computers is linked to the mathematics curriculum, the pupils working on computers will spend more time developing ICT skills than using ICT to explore mathematics. A major development activity for mathematics departments is to look for ICT possibilities within any topic being covered in classrooms, allowing the technology to be an integral part of mathematics learning rather than an add-on. Technology can offer valuable practice in mathematics and provides different environments for working on the same mathematics. Specific examples can be explored by those students who need to stay with special cases; others can explore their own hypotheses. The power of technology is that variables can be changed very easily, so you can challenge other students to test conjectures as they begin to generalise. One of the main things to be aware of is how the technology might change the mathematics and this is the first thing that we consider.

ICT and mathematics

The Framework specifically mentions LOGO, graphical packages and graphical calculators, geometry packages and spreadsheets. Many of you will have used LOGO and spreadsheets; fewer will have used graphical packages. There is a double-page spread of examples using graphical calculators in Years 7–9, but few schools will have the sets of graphical calculators that such work demands. The emphasis on geometry packages in the Framework will come as a surprise to many.

In order to show how the different packages affect the mathematics we will take one of the examples from the document and explore what happens when the task is completed using the different software. The example is a lovely question about constructing a square inside a circle and a circle inside a square (DfEE 2001: 4/15). The Framework suggests that pupils might use LOGO or a dynamic geometry package. The mathematics involved with the task could be very different with either of these packages. But the mathematics changes again if you use a graphical package or even a spreadsheet. We will consider the mathematics of the circle and square as they might be constructed using the different software packages and see what happens. You might like to have a go and compare your working with what follows.

LOGO is used mostly for drawing – sometimes called turtle geometry – using commands such as FORWARD (some units) BACKWARD (some units) RIGHT (an angle in degrees) LEFT (an angle in degrees). These instructions, or primitives, can be typed in and the turtle symbol will move on the screen after entering the command. More usefully the instructions can be collected into short programs called procedures, which can be given names and used for more complex drawings. The mathematics the software lends itself to most obviously is turn, angle (exterior), scale, bearings and constructing polygons, but it is a versatile tool and is designed for thinking mathematically. By devising procedures, you can develop the tools to shortcut the given processes. In terms of geometry you are always dynamically constructing the shape.

The square is constructed in LOGO by considering the path drawn as you trace the shape.

REPEAT 4 [FD 100 RT 90]

which can be acted out easily by pupils gives the locus of a square. Circles are drawn as many-sided polygons, so you may know the perimeter, but the size of the diameter is more problematic. The 'circle' in Figure 6.1, a 36-sided polygon, was drawn first, and then the square, but finding the size of the square is more of a problem.

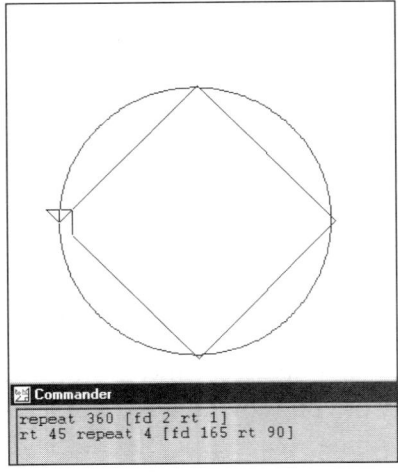

Figure 6.1 LOGO circle and square

Of course the task may be done so that it only looks as if the square is inside the circle. In LOGO that may be all that is possible, unless you approach it by constructing different polygons, say an octagon (Figure 6.2), then a 12- or 16-sided polygon; the mathematics is then changed and a lot of trigonometry could be involved. Or you could develop a sense of lengths of the sides of triangles.

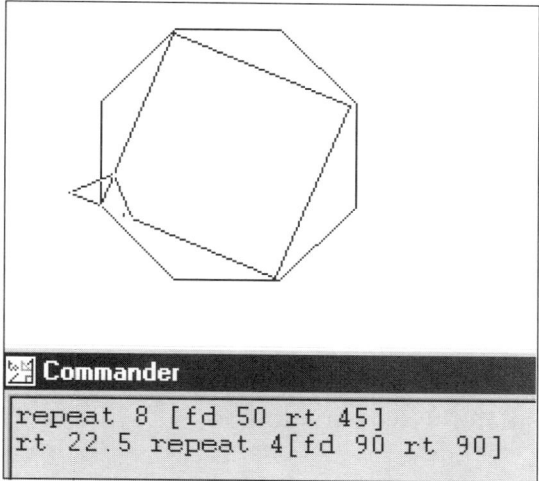

Figure 6.2 LOGO octagon and square

A geometry package, in contrast, offers construction of circles in different ways using line segments and perpendiculars. Transformations can be easily achieved by dragging to change the sizes of the shapes. You need to use different properties of the shapes you wish to construct (unless you use a polygon tool) from those in LOGO. In the geometry package, you can construct the square in a number of ways. Figure 6.3 used a circle, a ray and a perpendicular line to create a square with these two lines as lines of symmetry, given that the angle in a semi-circle is 90°. The mathematics of the constructions in a geometry package could include knowing:

- how to construct a square, perpendiculars, equal sides, etc.;
- that a square is a cyclic quadrilateral;
- that the angle in a semi-circle is a right-angle;
- that the diagonals of a square bisect each other at right-angles;
- that the diagonals of a square are lines of symmetry;
- that tangents to a circle are at right-angles to the radius at the point of contact.

Graphical packages offer the chance to plot coordinates (either Cartesian or polar) and draw curves from algebraic equations. To construct the square, properties such as equal sides and parallel lines or diagonals as lines of symmetry may be used to choose the coordinates to plot (or you might have a square centred on the origin using a polygon tool). Circles can be drawn using equations of the form $x^2 + y^2 = r^2$ (Figure 6. 4).

Other squares could be drawn, and you then have to decide on the level of accuracy you will accept for the coordinates. Or you could create the square from the intersection of lines, offering practice of parallel and perpendicular lines ($y = x$, $x + y = 1$, etc., as in Figure 6.5) as you explore different orientations of the square.

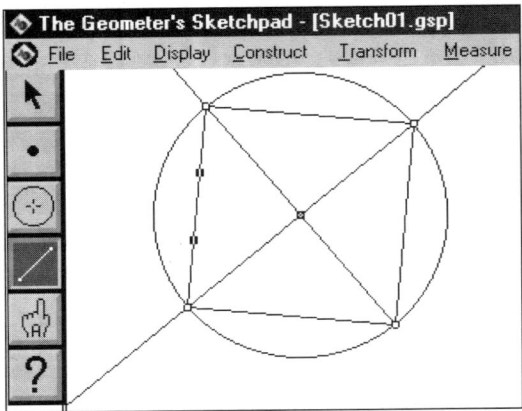

Figure 6.3 Geometer's Sketchpad circle, with diameters as lines of symmetry of a square

You may need to know that the equation of a circle is not a function of x, so that you have to enter (especially with graphical calculators) two equations:

$$y = +\sqrt{r^2 - x^2} \text{ and } y = -\sqrt{r^2 - x^2}.$$

You could, of course, be interested in using polar equations with your high achievers, which is another dimension that ICT offers you a chance to explore (Figure 6.5).

We use a spreadsheet to complete the analysis, which is an interesting mathematical challenge.

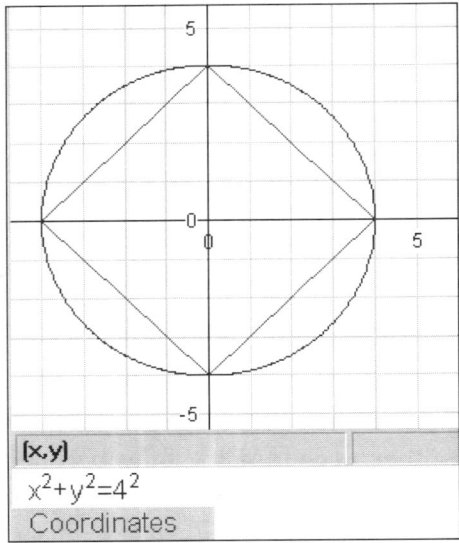

Figure 6.4 Omnigraph circle and square

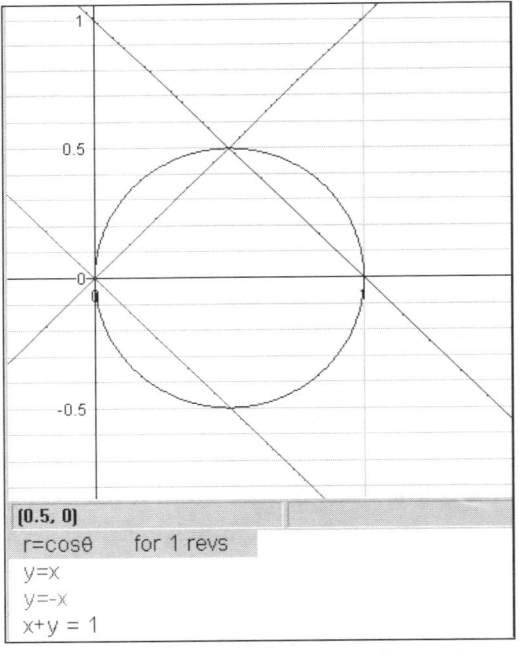

Figure 6.5 Omnigraph circle from the polar equation and lines forming a square

Spreadsheets can be adapted to draw coordinate diagrams, using the scatter diagram facility. You will need to be careful about the scale on the axes, because most work is done by dragging. The function notation is necessary for plotting the points of the circle, but you also have to decide how many points you want to plot to get an approximation of circle. Figure 6.6 shows the calculations for the polar equation $r = 5\cos\theta$ (the formulae need to use radians) and the related scatter diagram for the 'circle', with the coordinates for the square. You could, of course, use the theorem of Pythagoras (see Figure 6.12, p. 65). The choice of the mathematics is widened by the technology.

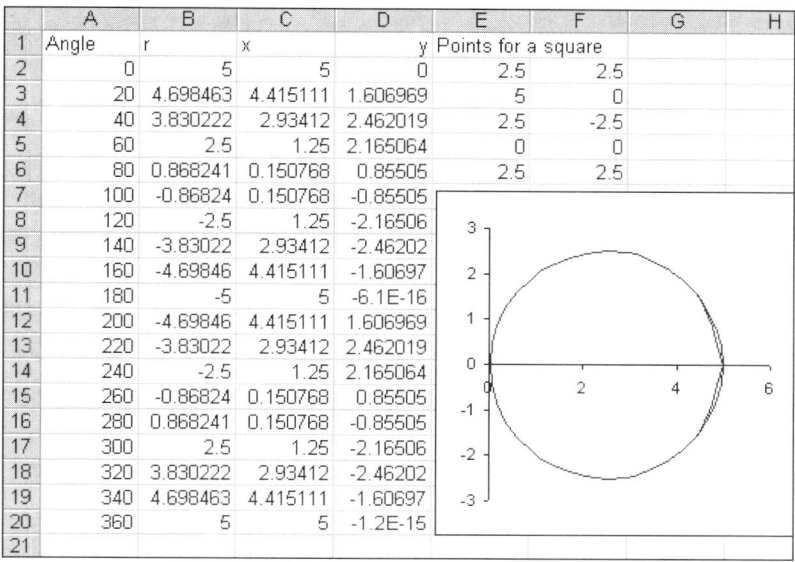

	A	B	C	D	E	F	G	H
1	Angle	r	x		y	Points for a square		
2	0	5	5	0	2.5	2.5		
3	20	4.698463	4.415111	1.606969	5	0		
4	40	3.830222	2.93412	2.462019	2.5	-2.5		
5	60	2.5	1.25	2.165064	0	0		
6	80	0.868241	0.150768	0.85505	2.5	2.5		
7	100	-0.86824	0.150768	-0.85505				
8	120	-2.5	1.25	-2.16506				
9	140	-3.83022	2.93412	-2.46202				
10	160	-4.69846	4.415111	-1.60697				
11	180	-5	5	-6.1E-16				
12	200	-4.69846	4.415111	1.606969				
13	220	-3.83022	2.93412	2.462019				
14	240	-2.5	1.25	2.165064				
15	260	-0.86824	0.150768	0.85505				
16	280	0.868241	0.150768	-0.85505				
17	300	2.5	1.25	-2.16506				
18	320	3.830222	2.93412	-2.46202				
19	340	4.698463	4.415111	-1.60697				
20	360	5	5	-1.2E-15				
21								

Figure 6.6   Excel and polar equation of a circle

Next we consider each of the software packages in turn and look at the demand for their use in the examples of Section 4.

Spreadsheets

Spreadsheets are the most mentioned ICT resource in the document. The specific content for which spreadsheets are recommended is shown in Table 6.1.

The 'Handling data' work is probably very familiar to you; spreadsheets were designed for such mathematics (some examples are given in Chapter 8). Spreadsheets such as Excel will construct all sorts of diagrams and care needs to be taken in their choice. You can also explore trend lines, moving averages, lines of best fit and so on. The danger can be that too much is available too easily; pupils need to learn to discriminate.

Textbook questions need to be changed for use with ICT to provide challenging mathematics as otherwise the task might be trivial. Sometimes the change might be more of the same, so that pupils can be asked to generalise from the special cases; sometimes the method of solution will change with the technology.

Table 6.1 Topics for spreadsheets

Year 7	Algebra	Entering formulae, generating data, tables of values, counting in steps, term-to-term, position-to-term
	Handling data	Storing and representing data
Year 8	Number	Direct proportion, inverse operations
	Algebra	Verifying identities, substitution, generating sequences, data for functions, transformation data
	Handling data	Calculating averages, storing data, representing data
Year 9	Number	Square roots, indices, testing properties
	Algebra	Solving equations, approximate solutions, generating sequences
	Space and shape	Trigonometric ratios
	Handling data	Calculating averages, statistics experiments, storing and presenting data, scatter graphs

For example, let's have a look at solving equations.

> Solve the equation $3x - 7 = 20$.

If pupils are at the first stages of solving equations you may want to look at 'trial and improve' as a method, and you might find that using bigger numbers in the equation attracts more pupil interest. You could devise a template, so that pupils type in numbers and the left-hand side of the equation is calculated. If you did this it would also be worth changing the 20 and asking pupils to solve several equations of the form $3x - 7 = ?$.

The difficulty lies in the mathematics the pupils are doing; if they are just entering numbers at random the exercise is purposeless. If they are getting closer to solutions and can explain how they are making their choices, they will be doing more mathematics. Working to a solution of $3x - 7 = 23$, once you have solved $3x - 7 = 20$, allows for a refinement of technique. Switching to solving $3x - 7 = -20$ moves the solution into negative numbers, requiring a different way of ordering numbers. It is in explaining and justifying the differences that the mathematics lies.

It is just as easy to solve equations involving powers of x in this way as it is to solve linear equations, so the method can be extended to something that has more value in the mathematical field. (Only linear and quadratic equations have easy algebraic methods of direct solution. That's why we learned them. But now we have the power of computers, so why not use a more general technique?)

The link to graphical solutions is easily made, and it may be easier to begin by solving simultaneous equations such as $y = 3x - 7$ and $y = 2x + 3$ (see Figure 6.7) and their like, before solving $3x - 7 = 20$ as the intersection of $y = 3x - 7$ and $y = 20$ (Figure 6.8). (We have shifted packages here, as a graphical package is better for looking at equations, and it would be easy to have both packages open.)

Alternatively, pupils could design their own formulae. If a cell or row/column is named as 'x' in Excel, you can use the x in the formulae, although you will have to add in all the operations.

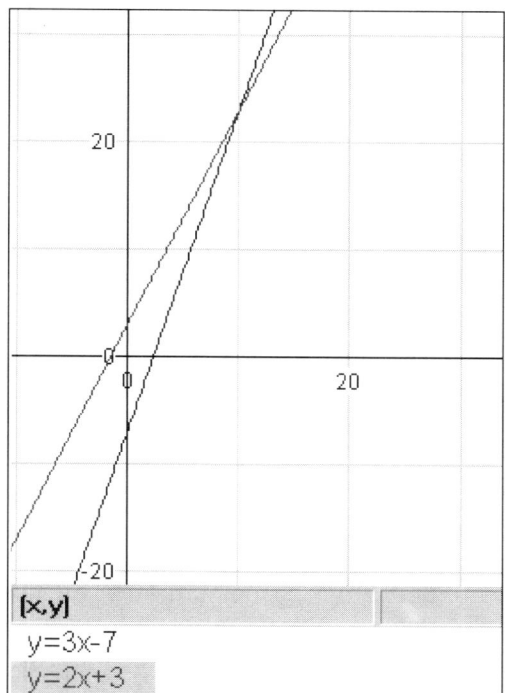

Figure 6.7 $y = 3x - 7$ and $y = 2x + 3$

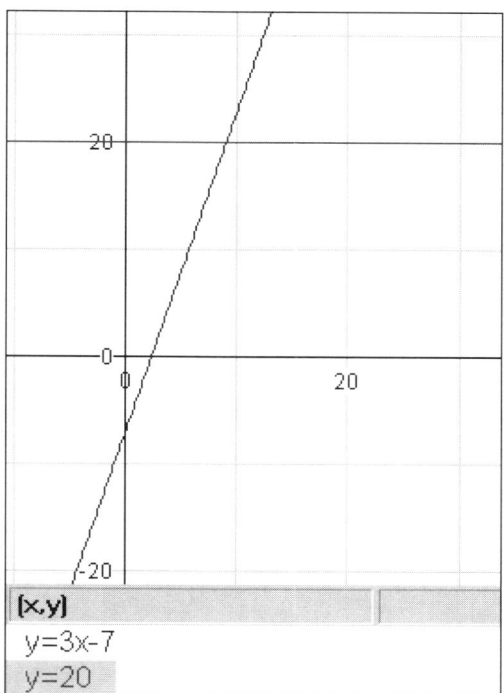

Figure 6.8 $y = 3x - 7$ and $y = 20$

Design several equations where $x = 4$ is a solution.

Or perhaps a better challenge might be:

Design several equations of the form $f(x) = 20$, where $x = 4$ is a solution.

So, for example, if cell A1 is named x, each of the formulae in cells B1 and C1 in Figure 6.9 would give 20 when you look at the normal version of the spreadsheet.

	A	B	C
1		x		
2	4	=3*x+8	=28-2*x

Figure 6.9 Spreadsheet for equations

The equations found so far are $3x + 8 = 20$ and $28 - 2x = 20$, both of which have the solution $x = 4$.

What else are spreadsheets useful for? The Framework example on entering formulae creates the opportunity to explore substitution.

Enter a formula such as 3A + B in column C.
Find six different ways of putting numbers in columns A and B to produce, say, 56 in column C. Try other formulae in column C.   (DfEE 2001: 4/138)

	A	B	C
1	2	4	$= 3 * A1 + B1$
2	3	4	$= 3 * A2 + B2$

Figure 6.10 Spreadsheet for substitution

Figure 6.10 shows a template. Neither pair of numbers gives success, but they may be necessary as pupils work towards a solution. More than six solutions can be found. But the mathematics is only exploited when the solutions are found not by trial and improve, but by looking at the connection between the numbers more explicitly.

Sequences are an obvious area where using a spreadsheet allows exploration but it is pointless asking pupils to find the next two terms of a sequence as you can drag and fill. Questions like the following one need to be adapted.

> Find the next two terms of the sequence: 3, 7, 11, 15, _ , _

In Excel you can type the 3 and 7 into adjacent cells, highlight them and drag to make a sequence as long as possible. No mathematics is required, just the ICT skills of highlighting and dragging. This can be changed into a more mathematical task by asking pupils to type different pairs of numbers so that the fifth term of the sequence is 19.

> Type in different pairs of numbers, and drag the sequence. The aim is that the fifth term of the sequence is 19. What are the rules for choosing the numbers?

Most spreadsheets will graph the data, so you can explore the pictures of the sequences with different starting numbers, but a common value as a set term. Figure 6.11 shows three sequences that successfully achieved a fifth term of 19. The scatter diagram that illustrates the sequences shows the ascending and descending clearly as well as the 'meeting', which was the constraint of the problem.

The pictures of the sequences now allow discussion of the terms 'discrete' and 'continuous'; for example why did we choose the diagram where the dots are not joined? The diagram may also lead into a discussion of the equations of lines that have the point (5, 19) in common, stressing the connections between the number in the

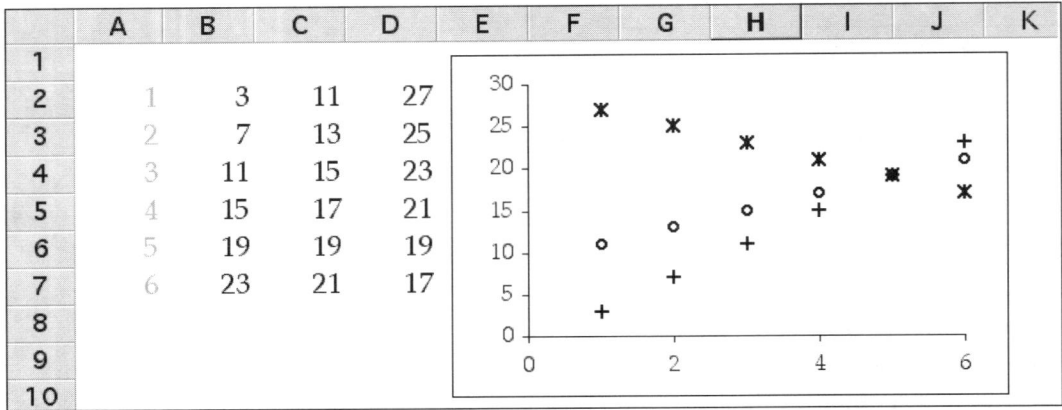

Figure 6.11 Dragging sequences

sequence and its position. Plotting sequences on a graphical calculator and then trying to determine the equation of the graph that passes through the points is another way of exploring this connection. (For more work on sequences using ICT, see Chapter 8.)

Graph plotters and graphical calculators

The Framework makes the suggestions for using these technologies; some are shown in Table 6.2.

Table 6.2 Topics for graph plotters

Year 7	Number	Number patterns, generating arithmetic sequences
	Coordinates	Drawing shapes
	Graphs	Working with $y = mx + c$
Year 8	Number	Number patterns, divisibility, square roots
	Algebra	Verifying identities
	Graphs	Drawing graphs, $y = mx + c$
Year 9	Number	Square roots, indices, plotting proportionality
	Algebra	Solving simultaneous equations, approximate solutions, iteration
	Graphs	Plotting graphs, sketching graphs, $y = mx + c$, $y = ax^2 + b$, $y = ax^3$

One advantage that graphical calculators have over ordinary calculators is the number of results that are visible on the display. Several results are visible at a time, and this allows exploration of sequences and number patterns in much the same way as with spreadsheets. The calculators were, of course, designed for the exploration of graphs in the same way as with many computer packages. The advantage of the calculators is that you are not in competition for the computer room. You can use them with your pupils at an appropriate time. When you are ready for the mathematics of a graph, calculators can be more accessible than computers. You can work with them at many different levels. Your low achievers can use their calculators to explore the relationships with graphs even if they have difficulty understanding substitution or plotting coordinates.

Typically, graph plotters plot graphs, so what kind of mathematics might be explored if the technology does the work of plotting a graph? Again, because of the speed of the 'plot', the software can be used to explore the consequences of changing variables in the equations of graphs (this can complement the work in spreadsheets but what is the difference in the mathematics?). What can a graph plotter do? And what can't it do?

Here are some suggestions.

> Plot $y = 2x$, $y = 2x + 5$ and $y = 2x - 3$.
>
> What is the same about these? What is different?

Pupils could explore $y = mx + c$, once they are used to changing the variables, but you might want to limit initial exploration.

Draw $y = ax$ for different values of a.

What happens?

Which lines pass through $(2, 4)$, $(2, 6)$, $(2, 10)$, $(2, 20)$, $(2, d)$ and $(2, 2p)$? Why?

Plot a series of lines that pass through the point $(4, 2)$.

This activity encourages pupils to explore parallelism of lines and the connection to the gradient of the line. Trying to form a rectangle moves the exploration to perpendicularity.

Plot the line $y = x$.

Plot 3 more lines so that the 4 lines surround a parallelogram.

When do you get a rectangle?

Can you plot lines so that they surround a rectangle of area 8 square units?

The task can be made easier by plotting a line such as $y = 3$, but the mathematics is more challenging if the shape is not orientated to the axes. Pupils can be challenged to draw a rhombus, a trapezium, a regular octagon; you can decide how hard the challenge might be.

You do have to be aware of the limitations of functions – why is it difficult to draw lines of the form $x = 4$? Calculators can appear very complex – too many buttons and menus – and software may not work in the way you expect it to. You test equations of lines by typing them in and seeing if they overdraw the line you are considering. You do have to use the limitations creatively.

Some packages allow you to transform lines using reflections, rotations, translations, etc. You can use these to provide more practice of identifying lines. If you use translations the gradient will remain the same and only the constant will alter, so parallelism is preserved.

Draw the line $y = x$, and translate the line 6 units to the left. What is the equation of the image line?

Repeat this with $y = 2x$, $y = 3x$, $y = 4x$, $y = 6x$, $y = -x$, etc.

What is the image of the line $y = ax$? Why?

Draw the line $y = x$. Reflect it in the line $x = 0$. What is the equation of the image line?

Repeat this with $y = 2x$, $y = 3x$, $y = 4x$, $y = 6x$, $y = -x$, etc.

What is the image of the line $y = ax$? Why?

What aspects of the line are preserved?

Dynamic geometry package

Table 6.3 Topics for dynamic geometry package

Year 7	Sketching diagrams, working on reflections and rotations Drawing squares
Year 8	Constructing triangles, parallelograms, transforming shapes, area
Year 9	Constructing, all polygons, transforming shapes, combining transformations, circle properties, using constructions

All the examples come from Ma3, Space and shape, as you would expect. Dynamic geometry packages are not yet used in many schools, but there is an increased emphasis in the geometry section of the Framework – more Euclidean geometry as well as proofs. One of the activities to have a go at for yourself if you are a newcomer to such packages is to construct a square that is always a square (and then replace the word 'square' with another shape). It is quite a challenge to construct, and there are many ways to construct it depending on which set of minimal conditions you might choose. Consider the ways this 'square' might be constructed and then analyse the resulting mathematics that you need to access. Our ideas at the beginning of this chapter suggest some of the possibilities.

The dynamic nature of the diagrams allows the geometry to be explored in ways that can help to reinforce the properties of shape.

> Draw two line segments that do not touch or cross. Construct a point of intersection on both segments and draw a third line segment joining these points.
> Mark and measure the angles shown and look at their size as you drag the original line segments.
>
> When are the original line segments parallel? How do you know?

Figure 6.12 shows one possible picture you obtain when you construct this in a geometry package. What it cannot show is the effect of the moving picture. The angles change as you move the points. Deciding that the lines AB and CD are parallel can happen in lots of different ways. Specialising and generalising is a function of these pictures. Proving parallelism is a different issue.

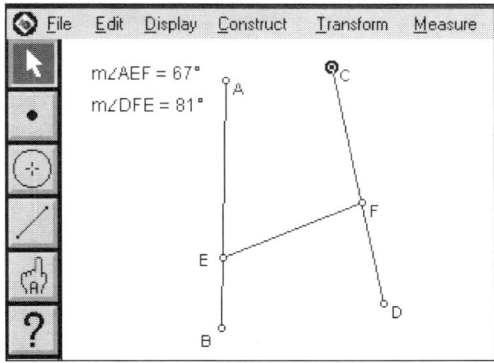

Figure 6.12 Three line segments

In Figure 6.4, the alternate angles were measured, but you could choose the corresponding angles or you could display the measurements of all of them to encourage pupils to make different conjectures. This activity can be done with geo-strips as well, but the angles then have to be measured.

Dragging could also help you to look at the properties of cyclic quadrilaterals.

Construct a circle and four points on the circumference. Join these points with line segments to form a quadrilateral. Mark the angles. What do you notice about the angles as you move the vertices?

Can you make your quadrilateral a trapezium? How do you know it is a trapezium?

Can your quadrilateral be a parallelogram, rhombus, rectangle or square?

Construct a circle and three points on the circumference. Join these points with line segments to form a triangle. Mark one of the angles. What do you notice about the angles as you move the vertex of the marked angle?

What happens if the other two points are on a diameter?

What happens if the three points are in a minor sector?

This dynamic way of finding the angle subtended by a chord, with the special case of the chord being a diameter, is likely to make these properties more memorable.

LOGO

Table 6.4 Topics for LOGO

Year 7	Geometry	Drawing regular polygons
Year 8	Algebra	Working with variables
	Space and shape	Generating shapes
Year 9	Shape and space	Constructing polygons, loci

The focus is yet again on shape and space, but LOGO can be used for number, so that variables can be used in both number and shape. Note that we are using the syntax of MSWLogo. Other versions will have different syntax. MSWLogo needs the 'STEP' procedure, whereas others offer different ways of pausing.

We will say something about variables in number first. LOGO allows a different focus on formulae, with the techniques of procedures calling themselves, which offers a wonderful sense of the inductive definition. For example:

SEQ :A
PRINT :A
SEQ :A + 7

If the procedure is entered, then typing SEQ 2 will cause 2, 9, 16, 23, 30, etc. to be printed. Mathematical questions that might be asked include:

- What different starting numbers can you use so that 50 is one of the terms?
- What different starting numbers can you use so that 73 is a term? or 21.5? or 6?

If you want the position of the term to be printed before the number, the procedure can be altered to:

SEQ 'N 'A
PRINT :N, :A
SEQ :N + 1 :A + 2

The geometrical images in LOGO might lead you to explore spirals or ray diagrams:

SEQ :A	SEQ :N :A
FD :A RT 90	FD :A BK :A RT 10
IF :A > 100 STOP	IF :N > 35 STOP
SEQ :A + 2	SEQ :N + 1 :A + 2

You can focus on geometrical images by designing procedures to test shapes.

Use the procedure

    SHAPE :A :B

    REPEAT 2 [FD 100 RT :A FD 70 RT :B]

When do you get a closed shape? Why?

The other way round

To complete this chapter we thought that we would look at the different technologies for the same mathematics, just as we did for the square and circle at the beginning. But this time we will also look at the consequences for the learner. What about the theorem of Pythagoras?

Pythagoras and spreadsheets

Any data collected from drawings of right-angled triangles could be checked against the theorem using a spreadsheet, but as access to computers often mitigates against drawing, you may be better doing this with one computer and testing the results as a class. This type of activity will need much discussion about error in measurement and ideas of 'best fit'.

Any other activity needs to test some type of hypothesis to offer purpose to the data.

It is said that if two consecutive numbers add up to a square number, the two numbers and the square root of the square number form a Pythagorean triple.

Test this by using a spreadsheet (Figure 6.13).

	A	B	C	D
1			SUM	
2	3	4	7	
3	4	5	9	3
4	5	6	11	
5	6	7	13	
6	7	8	15	
7	8	9	17	
8	9	10	19	
9	10	11	21	
10	11	12	23	
11	12	13	25	5
12	13	14	27	
13	14	15	29	
14	15	16	31	
15	16	17	33	
16	17	18	35	

Figure 6.13 Finding Pythagorean triples

Use a spreadsheet to find some values of the shorter sides of right-angled triangles when the hypotenuse is 20cm.

Draw a scatter diagram of these values. What happens? Why?

Figure 6.14 shows some possibilities. Why do you get something that looks like a quarter of a circle? How would you get some more points? This offers a different way of drawing a circle, before pupils meet the Cartesian equation. It also makes the equation much more obvious, especially when you move to $(x - a)^2 + (y - b)^2 = r^2$.

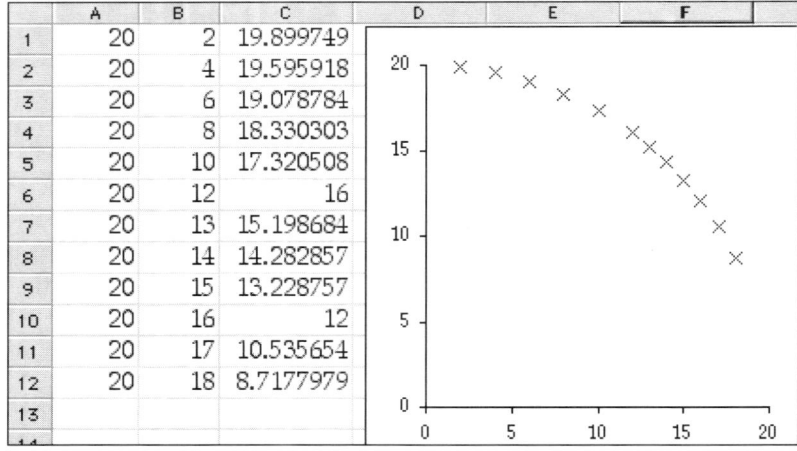

	A	B	C
1	20	2	19.899749
2	20	4	19.595918
3	20	6	19.078784
4	20	8	18.330303
5	20	10	17.320508
6	20	12	16
7	20	13	15.198684
8	20	14	14.282857
9	20	15	13.228757
10	20	16	12
11	20	17	10.535654
12	20	18	8.7177979
13			

Figure 6.14 Pythagorean trios where the largest is 20

Pythagoras and dynamic geometry packages

Find Pythagorean trios by dragging a right-angled triangle (see Figure 6.15).

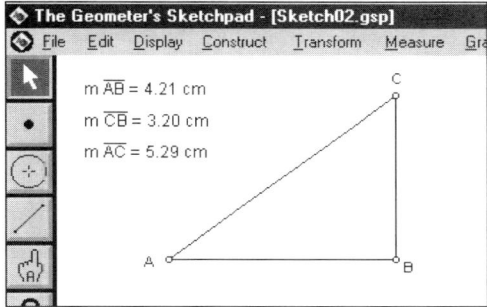

Figure 6.15 A right-angled triangle.

You could drag any triangle and use a spreadsheet to check the measurement if you think you have a right-angled triangle. Be prepared for discussion on error.

You may of course prefer to look at numbers with the length of the hypotenuse fixed (offering a comparison to the similar task using the spreadsheet above).

Drag the vertex at the right-angle of the triangle drawn in a semi-circle (Figure 6.16).

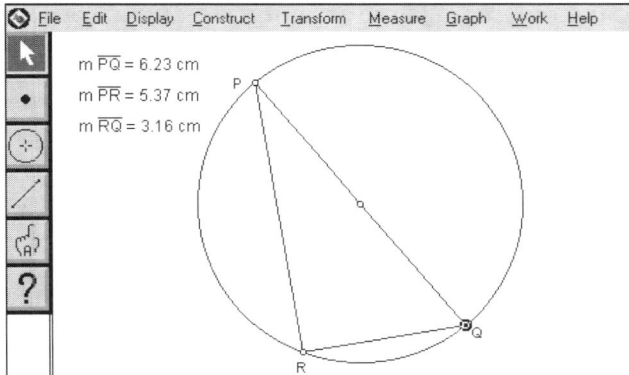

Figure 6.16 The triangle in a semi-circle

This reinforces the circle theorem as well as controlling one of the variables, which is a useful mathematical strategy.

Pythagoras and LOGO

> Find sets of numbers that make a right-angled triangle using the shape procedure in Figure 6.17.

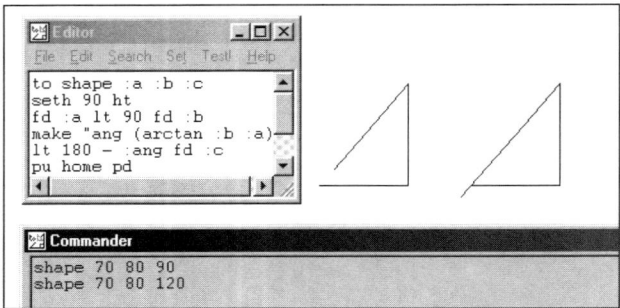

Figure 6.17 LOGO and the theorem of Pythagoras

This task looks similar to the one above, but it feels very different as you experiment. The geometry package starts with a completed triangle giving the measurements. This task asks you to try to get the triangle by typing in three lengths. This works more on the feel for the size of the hypotenuse; a sense of the relationship rather than formalising the theorem.

Pythagoras and graph plotters

Omnigraph will find the area of polygons, which is an aspect that can help the choice of task. The following tasks approach the theorem via the area of right-angled isosceles triangles.

> Draw right-angled isosceles triangles with $x = 0$ as the line of symmetry. Find their area (Figure 6.18).
>
> Use the area to find the lengths of the equal sides.
>
> Justify your results using the theorem of Pythagoras.

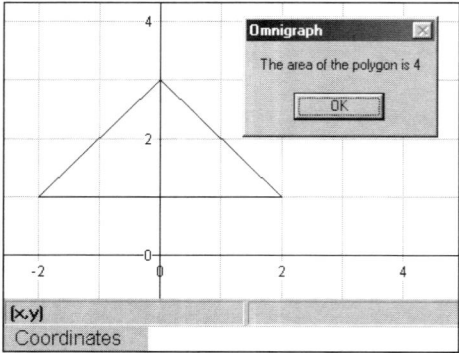

Figure 6.18 Isosceles right-angled triangles and area

This task connects symmetry and the area of triangles to the theorem of Pythagoras. We may also want to link equations of lines. You could also do this task with pairs of lines that bound the triangles, such as $y = 10 - x$ and $y = x + 4$. In Figure 6.18 you could consider the triangle as bounded by $y = 3 - x$ and $y = x + 3$.

The problem could be made more challenging by looking at the triangle in a different orientation.

Draw the lines $y = 4x$ and $y = -0.25x$, and use these to plot a right-angled isosceles triangle (Figure 6.19). Find its area.

Use the area to find the lengths of the equal sides.

Justify your answer by using the theorem of Pythagoras.

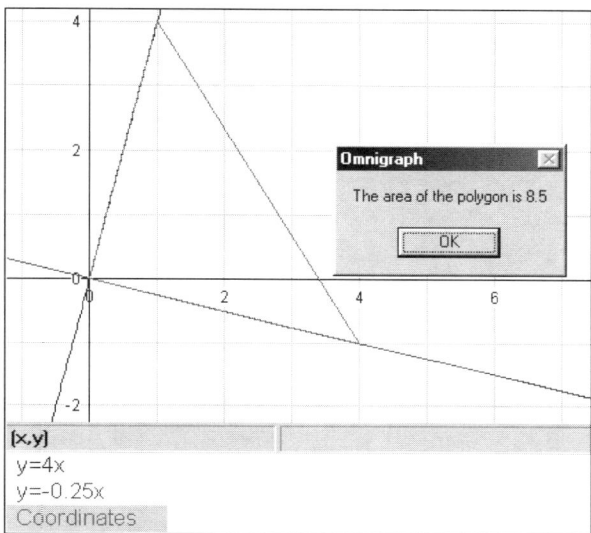

Figure 6.19 Lines, isosceles triangles and Pythaogras

Summary

In this chapter we have offered a review of the role of ICT in the Framework. There is a welcome emphasis on the place of ICT in mathematics, which is valuable if you are trying to improve your pupils' access to technology, but remember that calculators – four-function, scientific and graphical – are valuable in teaching mathematics. We have offered some examples of ways of using ICT (and there are more in Chapter 8, as this is still an area where examples are limited). The increased emphasis on geometry means that schools will need to use geometrical packages and to consider the links (Chapter 5) and the ways in which the different ICT packages can be related to offer wider perspectives of the mathematics.

ICT implies a different way of looking at the mathematics, but examinations have still not caught up with the implications of ICT. Drawing statistical diagrams seems an unnecessary skill, given that neater diagrams are quickly produced by ICT; the emphasis needs to be much more on the choice of the correct diagram and their interpretation.

Noss's recent evidence (1997) suggests that the widespread use of computers requires a workforce with a sophisticated understanding of the mathematical basis of models incorporated in software, rather than traditional computational skills, which are more quickly and accurately performed by machines (Brown *et al.* 1998: 365).

We do not claim that the examples above offer a 'sophisticated understanding' of the basis of the software used, but we would like to stress the need to exploit the mathematics as it suits the power of the software. Mathematics lends itself to ICT: ICT allows us to explore mathematics. The Framework supports the use of ICT in its documentation. The Framework becomes a powerful tool to persuade our budget holders of the needs of our learners.

7 Beginnings and endings

The quality of teaching is more important than class organisation, and this is broadly the message from research studies. More importantly we must try and make sure that, in spite of DfEE spin, teachers take the correct messages about what is important about the NNS: 'it's not whether it's whole class, group or individual teaching but rather what you teach and how you interact mathematically with children which seems to count.

(Brown 1999)

The oral and mental starter and the plenary are integral parts of the three-part lesson as described by the NNS. In Chapter 3 we discussed this lesson organisation where the three-part lesson was but one of many choices. So the question is, do we need oral starters at the beginning of each lesson and plenaries at the end of each lesson? What mathematical purpose do they serve? How might we plan their inclusion in some of our lessons? And what are the arguments when we choose not to use these formats?

Just as the NNS did not invent whole-class teaching or the daily mathematics lesson in primary school, so too it did not invent the three-part lesson. Every lesson has three parts, if we think of a beginning, a middle and an ending. The questions arise, what does the beginning look like, how does the lesson end and how many different parts is the middle divided into? Your beginning may be mathematical, but it might also be a management issue of getting pupils into the room, or settling them after a PE lesson. Your ending may be a formalised explanation of what the lesson was about, but it may also be about moving pupils to the next lesson. As a teacher you are always balancing mathematical needs with social demands and using structures to enhance learning as well as social relationships in the best possible way.

Beginnings – thinking ourselves in

Primary pupils who have worked with the NNS will be used to the idea of lessons beginning with an oral/mental starter with its emphasis on mental skills and recall. The role of mental methods (different from a mental starter) was discussed in Chapter 5, and their role in the NNS is clear from the Framework. But what about the starter or the warm-up? Certainly a starter will provide time to practise mental skills and techniques at speed. But there are other reasons for a starter and a long list is given in the NNS (DfEE 2001: 1/29) describing more than the rehearsal of skills. This list reflects three main purposes for such short activities for the learner:

- The frequent practice of facts, skills and vocabulary that need rehearsal, such as multiplication tables, number patterns and sequences, fractions/decimals/ percentages, number operations, conversion facts (100cm = 1m, etc.) and the use of formulae (e.g. area and perimeter of rectangle, algebraic substitution).
- Preparing for the rest of the lesson with short activities directly related to the content of the main teaching activity.
- Preparing for future learning; working for short periods on new material ready for later teaching activities.

What the NNS does not acknowledge are the management issues that sometimes confront the secondary teacher, who, unlike most primary teachers, might be changing classrooms through the school day and/or waiting for groups to arrive from different parts of the building. In these situations the starter might be a class management issue. We have spoken to teachers who would hate to lose those occasions when they have such a good main lesson planned that 'Good morning' is a sufficient starter, before they move straight into the main part. (Yes, despite what they believe in Whitehall, mathematics lessons can be exciting and an hour can be too short a time!)

Back to starters! The main questions to be answered are:

- What role will a starter play in this lesson?
- Where is the mathematics going?
- What purpose does the starter serve in the pupils' learning of mathematics?

Whatever the decision, the inclusion of such an activity should be as a result of intellectual planning for teaching and not as a response to an organisational audit. We then hit the problem of definition. There are hundreds of activities that could be used as a starter and many departments have already introduced them into the curriculum. These starters might be oral, mental or written or take the form of a discussion, with the same idea being used for oral work or for written work. The starters might be an adaptation of a main activity. You have to define the purpose. What we offer in this section are some suggestions for starters that might be used variously as a lead into the main part of the lesson, or as a reminder of yesterday's work or as a calming activity. Oh and by the way, you might use an oral activity in the middle of a lesson if this seems sensible. (Apologies if this seems obvious, but in these days of regulation and inspection a reminder that it's OK to act as an adult professional seems opportune!)

Additionally, the examples that follow offer a number of related practice tasks, which are connected in their mathematics content, so that, over a few lessons, the mathematical ideas can be linked and developed (links and connections are urged throughout the Framework). In this instance multiplication, multiples, expressions such as $3x$ and $5x$ and integer solutions to equations such as $5x + 3 = 13$ and $5x + 3 = 38$ are linked. The activities described can be done with flashcards or questions and answers, but some activities can be done making use of one computer – sometimes with just the monitor up high so that all can see, or better still attached to a television or electronic whiteboard.

Working in chorus with a purpose

One of the recommendations in the NNS for pupils learning English as an additional language is 'Encourage them to join in things that all pupils might do in chorus: extending a number sequence, counting along a decimal number line, chanting a multiplication table' (DfEE 2001: 1/35). This is advice that can be implemented usefully for all pupils. Chanting offers an environment where pupils can take a risk with their answers (knowing that their response is hidden in the crowd) or they can hear what others think, which may aid their learning. It can also hide the pupils who are not learning. This has led to the popularity of pupils having their own numbers cards, or fans or even a small whiteboard on which to write their own response and all the examples can be adapted to the use of such aids.

The following activities might be used discretely in time or planned to be used in a sequential way. Year 7 has as a key objective 'Use letter symbols to represent unknown numbers or variables' (DfEE 2001: 2/3), although many pupils will still be struggling to learn their multiplication tables. Working on a sequence of mental starters that link the ideas explicitly may help with both aspects.

Multiplication tables to expressions

> Shuffle flash cards, 0, 1, 2, . . . , 10. As you hold up a number, pupils respond with seven times that number.

Instead of flash cards you could use a random number generated by a spreadsheet on a computer screen.

- Use the idea to practise various times tables.
- Extend it, if appropriate, to ideas such as 'multiply by 3 and add 2' or 'multiply by 7 and subtract 1'.

Once pupils are used to the starter working on tables, you can adapt this to include some algebra.

> Add to the flash cards, 0, 1, 2, . . . , 10, some letter cards, a, b, c, d, e, g, k, x. Shuffle the cards. As you hold up a card, pupils respond with seven times that number or letter.

This activity offers a way of working on expressions without having to offer explanation. Once you get to ideas such as 'multiply by 3 and add 2', the ease of responding to letters can persuade your pupils that algebra is easy. You can also generate letters randomly on a spreadsheet – but you may find it easier to start with cards.

Substitution

Use the set of random numbers 0, 1, 2, . . . , 10 [(INT(RAND()*11)].

> Write the expression 2*a* on the board and write a sign saying '*a* =' to put on top of the monitor. The class chant the response as different random numbers are generated.
>
> Extend the activity to expressions such as 2*p*, 3*q*, 2*x*, etc.

Link these expressions explicitly to the multiplication tables.

- Extend the set of random numbers to –10, –9, . . . , 10 [i.e. INT(RAND()*21) – 10].
- Extend to expressions such as 2*a* + 3, 2*a* – 2, 2*a* = 0.5, etc.

If you are doubling, extend the set of random numbers to 0, 0.5, 1, 1.5, . . . , 9.5, 10 [i.e. 0.5*INT(RAND()*21)], which still gives integer chants, but moves into decimals and stresses the 'halfness' of numbers ending with '.5'.

- Work with decimals when using 10*a* [e.g. 0.1*INT(RAND()*21) – 1].

Solving equations

Use the set of random numbers 0, 3, 6, 9, . . . , 30 [3*INT(RAND()*11)].

> Write an incomplete equation on the board: 3*x* =
>
> Generate the right-hand side of the equation as a random number, so that pupils can chant the solution.
>
> | On board | On computer | Pupils chant |
> |----------|-------------|--------------|
> | 3*x* = | 27 | *x* = 9 |
> | 3*x* = | 12 | *x* = 4 |

Use the values for the right-hand side of the equation, which are multiples of 3, to make a link between the algebraic expression '3*x*', when *x* is an integer, 'multiples of 3' and the multiplication tables. This activity can be linked to the division process by using a multiplication grid.

The activity can be extended to equations that include another operation.

> Write an incomplete equation on the board: 3*x* + 7= . Generate the right-hand side of the equation as a random number, so that pupils can chant the solution.
>
> Use the set 7, 10, 13, . . . , 37 if you want whole-number solutions for this task [3*INT(RAND()*11) + 7].

The advantage of using a random number generator is that you can easily change the set of numbers to suit the level of work you want to do with your pupils. When particular sets of numbers are used you can begin to work on the generality of sets of numbers.

Other warm-ups

It can often be useful to warm up for a lesson, but not with an oral activity. Rehearsing conversions from metres to kilometres or centimetres may be a useful oral start for a lesson on scale drawing, but perhaps you want pupils to match cards, or fill in a table. You may want pupils to remind themselves of what happened in the previous lesson, by writing a short definition or talking in pairs. You may want to work on a short activity that allows you to move on to extend the practice of the mathematics. If you want a quiet start, perhaps a short written task could be useful.

Here is a written mental starter with another idea for working on algebraic substitution.

> Draw the diagram shown in Figure 7.1 on the board for pupils to copy as they come in. When everyone is settled, write a number in the middle for the pupils to work out the values at the end of the spokes.

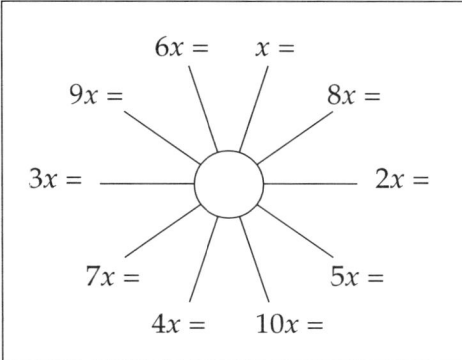

Figure 7.1 Polypede for substitution

The next part of the lesson could be extra practice, by changing the number, or an extension to the activity, by adding to the expressions (Figure 7.2). The structure allows you to exploit the connections between the differences and similarities.

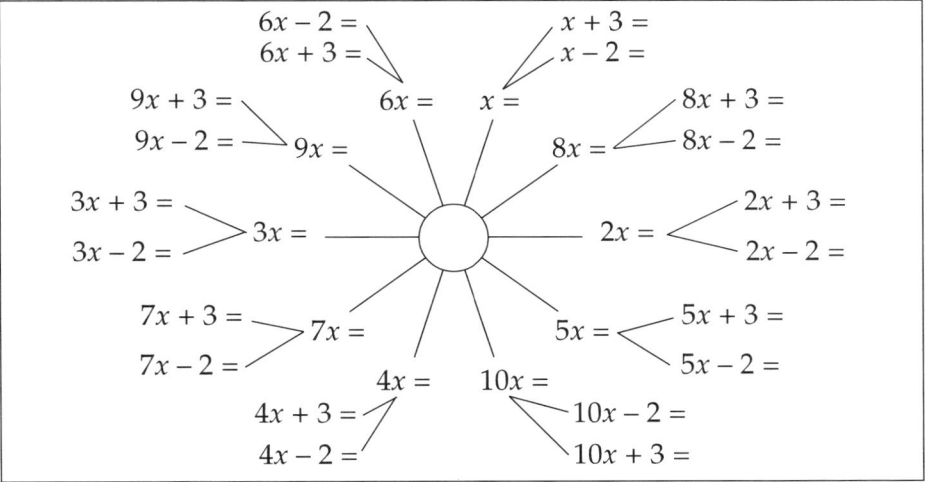

Figure 7.2 Extended polypede for substitution

Individual starters

Finally, some thoughts about class management. If your class tends to arrive late for whatever reason, the effect of the whole-class oral mental starter may be lost. You may want a different approach that challenges the personal achievement of pupils. Here are some ideas; no doubt you have many of your own:

- Have a multiplication grid to complete on each desk. Pupils complete the grid by the end of five minutes from the official start of the lesson.
- Keep a poster of results, questions completed, total correct, to encourage more prompt attendance.
- Start each lesson with a puzzle. Choose appropriate times to discuss solutions.
- Ask pupils to write down what they know about the topic of the lesson, ready to discuss it with others.

Endings: the plenary

The NNS has a very specific definition of the plenary.

> A final plenary to round off the lesson (from 5 to 15 minutes)

> whole-class work to summarise key facts and ideas and what to remember, to identify progress, make links to other work, discuss the next steps, to set homework.
>
> (DfEE 2001: 1/28)

The 'news reader' teacher image emerges from this definition as the most trivial interpretation of the plenary: tell them what you taught them. But it is your pupils who need to do the work; they need to do the learning. If you tell them what they did, it is unlikely that this will add to their learning. If they tell *you*, well something different is going on. Talking or writing about what has happened during a lesson may help the learning develop in different ways.

Fortunately, the NNS also offers some useful descriptions about using plenaries, which are worth discussing in departments.

> The plenary is an opportunity to round off and summarise the lesson, so that pupils focus on what was important, what they have learned and the progress they have made. It is a time when you can relate mathematics to their work in other subjects: for example, how their work on calculation will be used in science, or how their measuring skills will be practised in physical education or design and technology.

> You can use this part of the lesson to:

> - draw together what has been learned, summarise key facts, ideas and vocabulary, and stress what needs to be remembered;
> - generalise some mathematics from examples generated earlier in the lesson;
> - go through a written exercise pupils did individually during the lesson, so that you can question them about it, assess it informally and rectify any remaining misconceptions and errors;
> - make links to other work and what the class will go on to do next;

- highlight the progress made and remind pupils about their personal targets;
- set homework to extend or consolidate their class work and prepare for future lessons.

The plenary part of the lesson will be more effective if you:

- have a clear idea of its purpose and what you want to achieve in it;
- round off the lesson and evaluate its success.

(DfEE 2001: 1/30)

We now look at some of these in more detail.

The plenary as summary

- *round off and summarise the lesson*

Every lesson needs rounding off, even if this is only saying goodbye to your pupils, and having them say it to you; the courtesies make a huge difference to relationships in the classroom. Do you need to do anything more? Well, it depends. Rounding off a lesson may have different purposes, some of which we discuss below, from drawing together what has been learned to an ongoing task that pupils look forward to and can be used as a reward or sanction.

As for evaluating success, other than enjoyment, this is something that will need time out of the lesson and beyond the lesson, when books have been seen, when the topic is revisited. 'Teaching takes place in time; learning takes place over time' (Mason 1991). One lesson cannot be seen as divorced from the whole of the pupils' learning experiences. Any lesson has to be judged as a small part of a whole (which is why OFSTED evaluations seem odd, as they only judge on snapshots) and the teacher must consider the range of learning over a period of time.

- *draw together what has been learned*

Learning takes place over time, so in any one lesson it is unlikely that a teacher is going to know what has been learned. What is more important is helping your pupils to think about what they might have learned, by getting them to work on the ideas of the lesson. This suggestion in the definition of plenary, which can too easily be read as being for the teacher, is replaced with suggestions for activities for the pupils.

- *summarise key facts, ideas and vocabulary*

There are many different ways of working on summaries. The activities below stress the role of pupils in creating their own summaries. These will need to be discussed, but the teacher giving a summary rarely helps active learning.

> As individuals, write down 3 mathematical facts that you have looked at in this lesson. Share these with a partner and add to your list.

In a group of four, write down two sentences that describe the main ideas of this lesson.

Write a set of key word cards. Put the word on one side and write the definition on the other. Test each other in pairs by reading the key word and asking for the definition, or vice-versa.

Write key words and definitions in your mathematical dictionary.

Go round the class asking for a key word or definition.

Give a summary sheet with missing words for pupils to complete.

Go round the class asking for a summary sentence (it's OK to say 'My idea has already been used!').

Give two pupils the task of monitoring the lesson and reporting to the rest of the class what they think happened.

Homework: Describe the lesson and what you liked most about it (and least). Describe what you think you have learned.

- *stress what needs to be remembered*

It is sometimes useful to offer pupils reminders of what we need to remember: posters made by you or the pupils can offer useful reminders; language boards offer ways of focusing on important language.

Chant key phrases/relationships.

This can be extended to definitions, or even spelling; they are reminders.

Use acronyms as posters; for example, SGCC, specialise, generalise, conjecture, convince. Ask 'What were we doing when we specialised?' and so on.

Linking remembering activities to the labels of the processes can help to make the processes explicit as well as placing the activity into a mathematical context.

Homework: Make a poster to help us remember one aspect of the mathematics we did today.

This leads to a different starter – when the homework posters can be reviewed and pupils discuss why they thought certain aspects were important.

Does the plenary need to be at the end?

Let's look at some of the other aspects on plenaries offered in the NNS.

• *generalise some mathematics from examples generated earlier in the lesson*

This can be one of the most important aspects of sharing, and children's generalisations need to be shared at appropriate moments so that the mathematics can move on to explanation and proof. Always leaving generalisation to the end of a lesson can undermine the need to work on proof.

> On centimetre squared paper, draw some rectangles that are three times as long as they are wide.
> Write down what you notice about them.

The purpose of this activity is not to practise drawing rectangles, although some pupils will no doubt benefit from such a task, but to work on pattern in shape and connections to area and perimeter. If you were to wait until the end of a lesson to discuss the rectangle as a combination of three squares, the task would quickly become meaningless. The wording of the NNS must surely refer to an overall view of tasks that make up a lesson. In this case pupils might work on extensions to other rectangles (four times, twice as wide if appropriate) and a discussion of the connection to the usual formulae for area and perimeter of rectangles. The final plenary might then be a discussion of different findings. Or you may choose to leave pupils thinking about this for their homework and leave the discussion to the next lesson.

• *make links to other work and what the class will go on to do next*

Making links to other work needs to be an integral part of the teacher's work. Topics need to be linked back to work already done and forward to possible ideas. Lessons need to include:

- opportunities to rehearse previous work and to make links to the new topic;
- work on new ideas;
- development of a sense of where the mathematics might go.

Such opportunities need to be taken as appropriate. Leaving them to the end will waste the appropriate moments when links might be more memorable.

Other endings

The ending may be a plenary as defined by the NNS related to the main part of the lesson or you may need to use this time as a reward for good behaviour, as a potential sanction that allows you to remove what the class sees as a reward. Your class might enjoy a strategy game, or challenging each other to answer questions. The time allocated for such activities will depend on the class and the level of classroom sanction needed.

Play 1 to 10

All the pupils stand. Each pupil can say up three numbers, in order. The person who says 'ten' has to sit and the count begins again. For example, the game might go: '1, 2', '3, 4, 5', '6' '7, 8, 9', '10', so the fourth person forces the fifth person out.

Challenger

One pupil comes to the front (the winner from the lesson before), and another offers to challenge.

Both stand at the front and are asked a question. The first to answer the question correctly remains to be challenged by another. The loser sits down.

Although Challenger appears to involve only two pupils, when observed most pupils are involved. And although girls may not volunteer to challenge they get just as excited about answers.

Such activities seem to offer pupils a point to look forward to (rather than the bell). Classes can often be settled with a 'we will not have time to play . . . unless you get on with . . . ', which is a more gentle sanction than another detention. But they do not appear to fit the NNS philosophy. These activities can be justified on many levels, not just class management; strategy games can help mathematical thinking and planning ahead.

You may want your class to line up ready for the next lesson. This offers a good opportunity to practise some ordering.

Use a set of decimal cards. Pupils have one each and line up in order of the value of the decimals.

You can watch the discussion as pupils help each other sort the numbers, and the level of difficulty is easily organised to suit different classes.

Use a set of fraction, decimal and percentage cards. Line up in order of value.

This offers a different way of practising equivalence; different activities can suit different learners.

Have a set of shapes, and line up in order of the numerical value of the area or perimeter.

Getting ready to go can add a dimension of haste, created by the pupils themselves, and some learners learn by moving. Moving yourself into order can give a strong feel to the mathematical ordering.

These activities are all part of the experienced teacher's repertoire; we must not lose them because of externally imposed structures. You, not an external document, are the expert on what your learners need. Plan for them.

Summary

The NNS has placed much greater demands on mental methods and oral work and there is no doubt that this has not been over-emphasised in secondary schools. There is evidence that many primary pupils enjoy this part of the lesson. We do need to consider their role in our lessons. Brown *et al.* believe that 'More practice in mental and written calculation . . . will indeed improve English performance in number items in international tests' but they offer the warning, 'the price of improved performance in international number tests could well be a decrease in performance of mathematics in practical problem-solving, in other areas of mathematics and in other subject-areas, like science' (1998: 367). They agree that there is a consensus that improved oral and mental skills are essential for numeracy, but argue that 'discussion of the detailed balance of curriculum priorities has not been overt'. As teachers of mathematics, it is important that we balance the demands of the NNS with the needs of our learners. Oral and mental starters and plenaries can be useful, but only if we see them in relation to the mathematical learning that we hope our pupils will achieve.

The NNS offers mixed images of both the starter and plenary. As we have shown there are even more ways of using these types of activities. Teaching and learning are interactive and dynamic; they cannot be constrained by structures. As a professional you can choose:

- the form of the start of your lesson;
- the role of oral and mental work, when they happen and for how long;
- the place of plenaries, when you work with the class as a whole and their place in the mathematics;
- how you help learners to realise key points and important concepts;
- how you end your lesson.

We are aware of the pressures to conform; it can make it easier for the senior management team to account for compliance to national initiatives. If you have the language to describe the purpose of your activities, how your lesson begins and ends and why, you can make yourself less vulnerable to such pressure. The activities described here only offer a flavour of the many possible choices you can make; you will have many more.

8 Planning for teaching: using the examples

The examples in Section 4 of the Framework are presented as a double-page spread, with columns of examples for each of Year 7, Year 8 and Year 9. They are intended as guides to an interpretation of the mathematical objectives as well as representing assessment outcomes at the end of each year. As teachers, we are familiar with looking at examples; every time they change the GCSE and A-level syllabuses we wait to look at the specimen papers. All of us use last year's papers to help our pupils to prepare for next year's examination, but we do not teach to these papers. We use the examples to help pupils to practise passing the examinations. The examples and mathematics we do in our classroom will sometimes look like the examination questions, but we also need to use examples that extend the thinking of our pupils so that the examinations appear easy. We do not need to talk about using the examples for practice. But what about using the examples for planning for teaching and learning? An alternative to practice is to use the examples for thinking about the mathematics, about possible routes through the mathematics and for thinking about ways to create activities for the classroom.

In this chapter we look at the some of the examples from Section 4 as ways of helping planning for the main teaching activity. Clearly, there is only room in this chapter to work on a few of the examples but we hope we offer sufficient examples for you to work with other aspects of the Framework with your department.

Using the examples

One of the major advantages of the presentation of the examples in the Framework is that the examples related to the objective for Year 7, Year 8 and Year 9 are side by side (described in Chapter 2). This makes it easier to look at the possible routes to the assessment at the end of Year 9. The questions give ideas for classroom activities as well as ensuring that we use the language and conventions that will be included in the SATs in Year 9.

Each objective in Years 7–9 is accompanied by at least one double-page spread, illustrating the type of assessments that might be used for pupils. To use these for planning we have constructed a four point plan:

1. Take one double-page spread and look at how the objective is described for each year, consider any differences and decide whether your planning for Year 7 needs any aspects of the objectives from Year 8 and Year 9 and if Year 8 needs any of

Year 9. You may need to look back at Section 3, the yearly teaching programmes, to see if there is any more detail that can help.

2. Analyse the examples for Year 9 for interpretations of the objective.

3. Look in preceding years to see if there are examples that work towards those in Year 9. If not note where you need more ways of working towards Year 9.

4. Devise activities that allow you to work forwards and backwards in the mathematics.

This model may have to be adapted for particular sets of double pages. Sometimes interpretations of the objectives for Year 7, Year 8 and Year 9 are not given at the top of the relevant column – they are spread through the column and related to individual examples – or the Years 7–9 objective in the first column is not split up for the separate years.

Given the proviso that some adaptation is necessary, we will use these four points to consider three sets of examples from Ma2–Ma4 (and where we can we will also exploit ICT). You can question the results and debate whether the activities are useful. The choice of pages was arbitrary.

Shape, space and measures: geometrical reasoning: lines angles and shapes

1. Take the double page spread, 178–9

The objective for this aspect of mathematics is 'Use accurately the vocabulary, notation and labelling conventions for lines, angles and shapes; distinguish between conventions, facts, definitions and derived properties' (DfEE 2000b: 4/178). The teaching objective for Year 7 is 'Use accurately the notation and labelling conventions for lines, angles and shapes' and the language of 'distinguish between conventions, facts, definitions and derived properties' does not appear until Year 9. Yet this language could sensibly be used in Year 7, given that there are conventions for labelling lines and angles as well as definitions of shapes. Pupils in Year 7 will no doubt be working on derived properties. Imagine if pupils were expected to justify findings, such as explaining why the shape they have drawn by plotting coordinates is a rhombus. Such a justification or proof could use equal sides, or two lines of symmetry or diagonal crossing at right angles. Eventually properties will be explored and connected.

2. Analyse Year 9 examples

As stated above, the setting out of the examples tends to take different forms depending on objectives. The examples for Year 9 for this objective are accompanied by definitions of the language used in the Year 9 objectives and given here in Table 8.1.

In order to understand the way the Framework was using these terms we had to look closely at the published examples, comparing the ideas side by side (Table 8.2).

We have difficulty with the place of facts in this set of labels and could easily put the examples given as facts as examples of derived properties. There is also the

Table 8.1 Framework definitions of conventions, definition and derived property (DfEE 2001: 4/179)

A **convention** is an agreed way of illustrating, notating or describing a situation. Conventions are arbitrary – convenient alternatives could have been chosen.

A **definition** is a minimum set of conditions needed to specify a geometrical term, such as the name of a shape or a transformation.

A **derived property** is a fact, not essential to definition but consequent upon it.

Table 8.2 Framework examples of conventions, definitions and derived properties

Conventions	Definitions	Derived properties
The ways in which letters are used to label angles and sides of a polygon	A polygon is a closed shape with straight sides	A square has diagonals that are equal in length and that bisect each other at right angles
The agreement that anticlockwise is taken as the the positive direction of rotation	A square is a quadrilateral with all sides and all angles equal	Opposite sides of a parallelogram are equal in length

circularity of the definitions and derived properties. 'The diagonals of a rhombus bisect each other perpendicularly' is a derived property if the rhombus is defined as being 'a quadrilateral with four equal sides'. But I could define the rhombus as a quadrilateral with diagonals that bisect at right angles. Then the fact that the rhombus has four equal sides becomes a derived property.

3. Look at Year 7 and Year 8 examples for links

The examples in Year 7 use the language of the objective for Year 9 'the labelling convention for triangles'; they also offer definitions for line segment, angle, etc. This implies that you will need to work with the language of convention and definition at the very least. In Year 8 the objective begins 'Continue to use accurately the notation and labelling conventions', but the only example offers definition of interior and exterior angles of a triangle.

4. Devise activities

The ideas that have been noted in points 1–3 begin to start us thinking about ideas to use in the classroom to work towards the mathematics identified. Drawing in LOGO, for example, is related to exterior angles. When your Year 7 pupils are using LOGO you can build on their understanding of the language of interior and exterior angles as they work on constructing shapes in this particular environment.

Draw some different quadrilaterals.

Print some examples of LOGO drawings of different quadrilaterals. Make sure you record the instructions that you used to draw the shapes. Measure the angles.

Which are the interior and exterior angles? Are there any connections?

Print some LOGO drawings of triangles. Make sure you record the instructions you used to draw them. Measure the angles.

Which are the interior angles and exterior angles?

With a geometry package you can begin the explore the relationship between the interior and exterior angles in a dynamic situation.

Using a geometry package draw a triangle with one side extended. Mark and measure the interior and external angles (Figure 8.1). Drag the shape to change the angles. Record the different angles. What is the relationship?

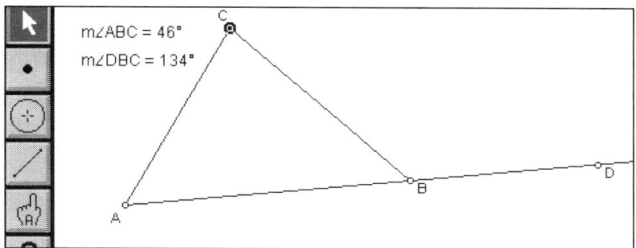

Figure 8.1   Geometer's Sketchpad triangle

As you drag a point, the measurements will change but the relationship should be constant.

Using a geometry package draw a quadrilateral. Label the interior angles.
Drag the shape to form different quadrilaterals. When do you know you have a parallelogram? When do you know you have a kite?

You can also explore the properties of shapes by seeing how different conditions imply a limited choice of shapes.

Using a geometry package draw two line segments that are perpendicular to each other. Join the ends of the line segments to form a quadrilateral with these line segments as diagonals. What quadrilaterals can you get by dragging (e.g. Figure 8.2)? Why?

Using a graphical package plot the points (2, 0) and (–2, 2). Draw in the mirror line that makes the points mirror images of each other. Plot two points on this line. Join the points to form a quadrilateral (e.g. Figure 8.3). What quadrilaterals can you form? Why?

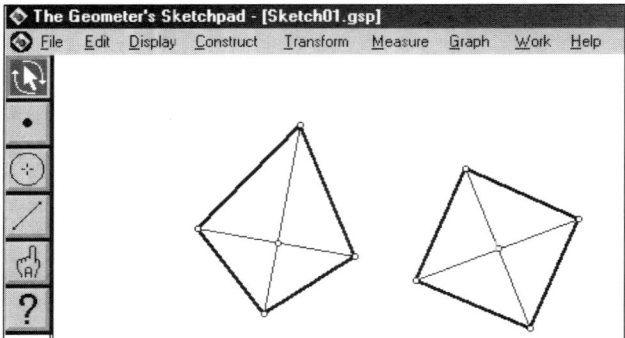

Figure 8.2 Geometer's Sketchpad perpendicular diamonds

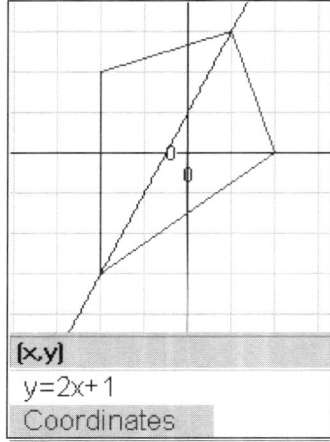

Figure 8.3 Omnigraph reflection and quadrilaterals

This last example offers practice across a range including coordinates and symmetry. Asking for the equation of the mirror line makes the link to algebra stronger.

Algebra: generating sequences

1. Take the double page spread 144–5

The objective is given as 'Generate and describe sequences'. In the teaching programme the Year 7 objective is 'Generate and describe simple integer sequences', and the Year 8 objective differs very little: 'Generate and describe integer sequences'. There are no examples given for Year 9, but there is an interpretation of the objective for the year. To look for indications of progression it is useful to consider the headings of each column of examples on these pages (Table 8.3).

The language offers aspects on which we can focus. It gives a sense of the progression the Framework is implying, with Year 9 expecting to be assessed on quadratic sequences.

Table 8.3 Headings of columns – language for sequences

Year 7	Use, read and write, spelling correctly: *sequence, term, nth term, consecutive, rule, relationship, generate, predict, continue, . . . increase, decrease . . . finite, infinite* (DfEE 2001: 4/144)
Year 8	Use vocabulary from previous year and extend to: *difference pattern, general term,* T(n) *. . . flow chart . . . linear sequence, arithmetic sequence . . .* (4/145)
Year 9	Use vocabulary from previous year and extend to: *quadratic sequence . . . first difference, second difference* (4/145)

2. Analyse the Year 9 examples

This is not possible, as there are no examples. (The best laid plans . . . !)

3. Look at Year 7 and Year 8 examples for links

The examples differ very slightly. The focus seems to be on developing language and using harder numbers, but there are important conclusions to the columns of examples (Table 8.4).

Table 8.4 Conclusions to examples

Year 7	Begin to categorise familiar types of sequence. For example: • sequences can be ascending (the terms get bigger), or descending (the terms get smaller); • some sequences increase or decrease by equal steps; • some sequences increase or decrease by unequal steps.
Year 8	Begin to appreciate that: • seeing a pattern in results enables predictions to be made, but any prediction must always be checked for accuracy; • a satisfactory conclusion is reached only when a general explanation of either a term-to-term or a position-to-term rule is given and the pattern can be justified.

4. Devise activities

Pupils have to work on the language of sequences and the standard practice rarely offers the opportunity to do this. Working on:

Find the next two terms of these sequences: 3, 6, 9, 12, __ , __ and 2, 5, 7, 12, __ , __

does not offer much opportunity for pupils to discuss what they are doing. If we open up the task the same two sequences may emerge, but so will others.

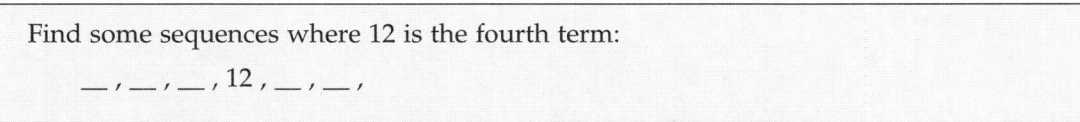

Each person's ideas are likely to be different from their neighbours'. As pupils swap ideas and sequences, they may share the rules of their sequences as they try to convince others of the correctness of the solutions. Explaining to the class can become a necessary part of the task as individuals try to show others their thinking.

Creating different sequences from the first two terms also means that the rules have to be explained to justify the responses and these rules will not all be linear.

> Find some different sequences that begin 1, 4 and give the rules for their generation.

An advantage of this type of activity is that it can be planned for without any awareness of the needs of individual learners. The activity is easy to explain and new examples can quickly be produced. Pupils can make the sequences as difficult or as easy as they wish. The most able children will work on collecting many different sequences, extending their mathematical ideas, while the teacher can work with those who need it (as can your able children).

Playing games can provide practice with discussion and sequence tasks can be changed into games.

Game for 2–4 players

Resources: Number cards (36)

Each player has 7 number cards. Each player is trying to create a three-term and four-term sequence.

Game for 2 or more players

Resources: Number cards plus blank cards (30)

Each player has 6 number cards and two blanks. One number card is placed face up. The first player puts down a card, explaining the sequence relationship. The next player continues, either by continuing the sequence or creating a new one. Blanks can be used to block a sequence.

The player who lays down all six number cards first is the winner.

There may be occasions when you want to work more particularly on the needs of other aspects of your pupils' learning. Supposing your Year 7 class consists of Level 3 children who are still having difficulty with learning their tables. Your work on integer sequences can focus on these.

A printed multiplication grid (Figure 8.4) allows you to work on the term and its position in the sequence, and this can be easily related to

$$1 \times 7 = 7$$

$$2 \times 7 = 14$$

$$3 \times 7 = 21$$

$$4 \times 7 = 28$$

where the first number gives the position in the sequence, the second the difference between terms and the third the number in the sequence. By working on the familiar (if unlearned) multiplication tables in an unfamiliar context you will be working towards the teaching objective at Level 5, but also allowing your pupils to learn more about the multiplication tables.

×	1	2	3	4	5	6	7	8	9	10	11	12	13	14	15	16	17	18	19
1	1	2	3	4	5	6	7	8	9	10	11	12	13	14	15	16	17	18	19
2	2	4	6	8	10	12	14	16	18	20	22	24	26	28	30	32	34	36	38
3	3	6	9	12	15	18	21	24	27	30	33	36	39	42	45	48	51	54	57
4	4	8	12	16	20	24	28	32	36	40	44	48	52	56	60	64	68	72	76
5	5	10	15	20	25	30	35	40	45	50	55	60	65	70	75	80	85	90	95
6	6	12	18	24	30	36	42	48	54	60	66	72	78	84	90	96	102	108	114
7	7	14	21	28	35	42	49	56	63	70	77	84	91	98	105	112	119	126	133
8	8	16	24	32	40	48	56	64	72	80	88	96	104	112	120	128	136	144	152
9	9	18	27	36	45	54	63	72	81	90	99	108	117	126	135	144	153	162	171

Figure 8.4 Multiplication grid

The grid in Figure 8.4 also offers lots of sequences that are not arithmetic. Just look at the diagonals. There are sequences such as:

4, 10, 18, 28, 40 . . .	increasing
42, 30, 20, 12 . . .	decreasing
8, 14, 18, 20, 20, 18	increasing then decreasing

There's plenty to explore with difference tables!

The progression for work on sequences is working towards quadratics. The multiplication tables give you plenty of these types of sequences to explore. At the same time you can rehearse multiplication and division as you extend the use of the grid to more complex sequences.

Given that pupils are expected to use ICT, they will probably develop all types of sequences. Linear sequences can be dragged in Excel or generated by formulae. Once sequences begin to be added, we get into quadratics, as with the sum of the integers or odd numbers (Figure 8.5). Pupils in Year 7 can explore these, before we formalise the work in preparation for assessment in Year 9. Excel can also draw the graphs to help pupils discuss the properties of sequences.

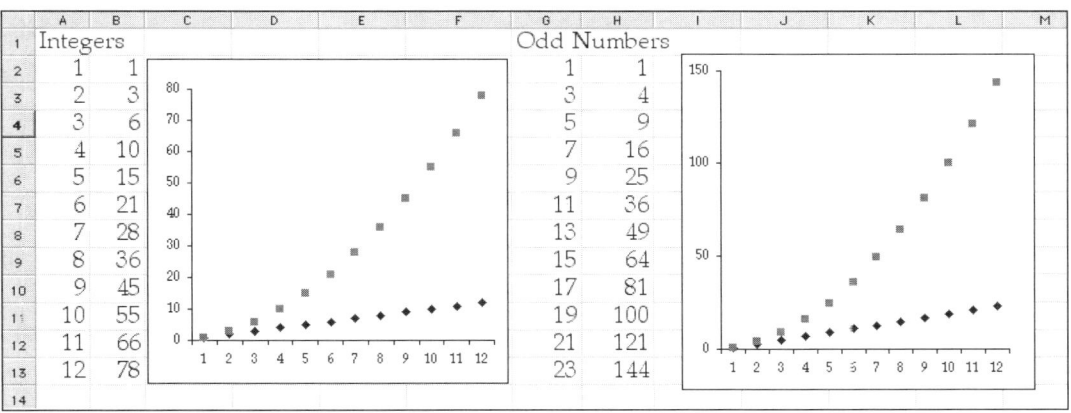

Figure 8.5 Using Excel for sequences and series

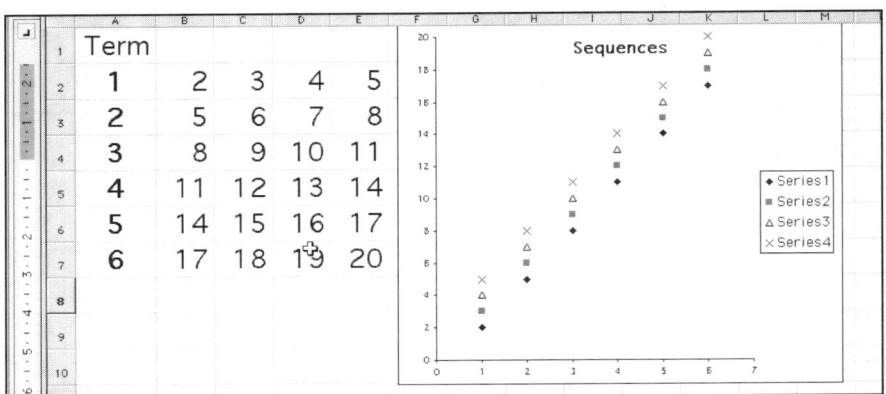

Figure 8.6   Add 3 sequences

As we work with arithmetic sequences, the diagrams allow us to explore when the sequences give us points on parallel lines. The arithmetic sequences in Figure 8.6 have been generated by the common difference of 3. By discussing the images generated by the spreadsheet you can begin to work on ideas of gradient and parallelism at the first stages of exploring sequences with ICT.

This type of diagram also allows ways of describing the categorising of sequences. What happens if you look at the sequences on the multiplication grid?

Handling data: calculating statistics from data

1. Take the double-page spread 256–7

The objective is 'Calculating statistics from data, using ICT as appropriate'. The objectives in Section 3 are given for more pages but the parts that are related to these particular pages of examples are given in bold in Table 8.5. The median is dealt with on the next double-page spread.

Table 8.5   Objectives for pages 256–7

Year 7	**Find the mode of a small set of discrete data.** **Calculate the mean** for a small set of discrete data, using a calculator for a larger number of items.
Year 8	**Find the modal class of a set of continuous data.** **Calculate the mean** for a large set of data, using a **calculator** or **spreadsheet**.
Year 9	**Select the statistics most appropriate to the problem.** Decide which of the measures of average is most suitable in a particular case, choosing between the median and the mean partly on the basis of whether extreme or chance values will influence the measure unduly. Be aware that the difference will be most significant in skew distributions, where both may need to be quoted. **Find the modal class of a large set of data.** **Calculate an estimate of the mean** of a large set of grouped data to a suitable degree of accuracy using a **spreadsheet**, or x, f facility on a **calculator.**

The median is dealt with on the next double page spread.

2. Analyse the Year 9 examples

The examples show a population pyramid (liaison with the geography department would be useful) to find a modal class and estimation of mean for intervals such as $0 \leq$ time ≤ 30, $30 <$ time ≤ 60, $60 <$ time ≤ 90, and age 10–19, 20–29, . . . , 80+

3. Look at Year 7 and Year 8 examples for links

The examples are directly related: mode of a very small set of numbers and a modal class and mean of a small set of numbers and from a frequency table. The progression lies in the difficulty of the examples, and particularly in the move to continuous data. No example in the Framework offers a way of working towards selecting appropriate statistics (nor is there one on the following pages).

The calculations of mode and mean are explicitly staged (although there are huge questions in our mind as to the need for estimated means in an age cf ICT). The major teaching issue is how to develop in our learners the skills to select the appropriate average, given that most of our texts focus on their calculation, rather than their purpose. This is clearly an area that requires discussion with those teaching citizenship, geography, history, economics, etc., so that real data and real purposes for such data can be used.

4. Devise activities

Spreadsheets offer the most obvious ICT for working on these objectives, although there are statistical packages that can be worth exploring. You can use the statistical facilities built into the spreadsheet or use the formulae to customise your worksheet. Developing a sense of number may be more important than using the formula for finding the mean, given that anyone who works with statistics will be using a computer, rather than worrying about the form of the formula.

Find sets of five numbers whose mean is 13.

	A	B	C	D	E	F
1		Set of Numbers				Mean
2	12	13	13	13	14	13
3	10	12	13	14	16	13
4	0	13	13	13	26	13

Figure 8.7 An Excel spreadsheet for finding means

Figure 8.7 shows a possible template that can be set up with pupils. The formula in F2, =AVERAGE(A2:E2), can be copied down column F. Excel will also find the mode and median, so this could be part of the sheet.

The task can be extended to different numbers of numbers, or different values of the mean:

- Ask for a mean of 13 but a mode of 11.
- Ask for a mean of 13 but a mode of 8.
- Ask for a mean of 13 and a median of 12.
- Ask for a mean of 13 and a median of 16.
- Are any related values of mean and median impossible? Why?
- Are any related values of mean and mode impossible? Why?

This task can be extended to finding the mean using frequency tables.

> Using the template in Figure 8.8, change the frequencies so that the mean is 5.

You can protect your template so that pupils cannot change any of the other numbers. Whether or not the diagram should have gaps between the bars is an argument we might have with Microsoft!

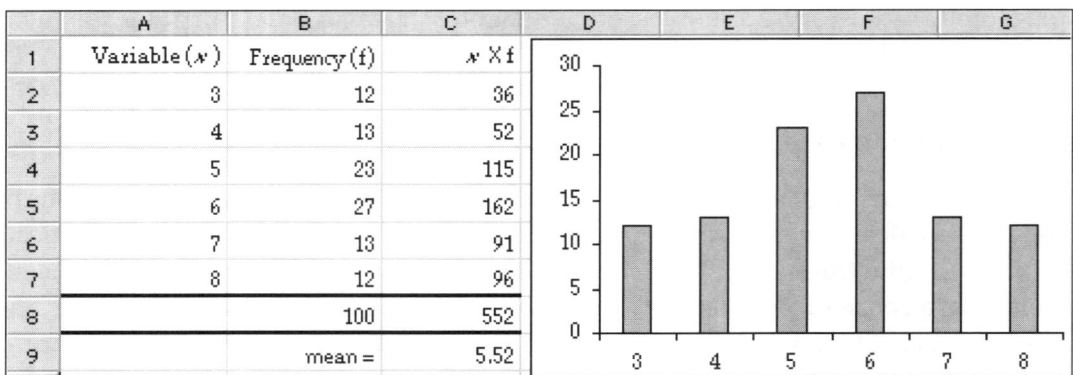

Figure 8.8   Excel template of a frequency table

What are the strategies you might use to solve the problem? Symmetry? Patterns of numbers? Does it matter if you change the total frequency?

- Can the mean be 7?
- Once you have a mean of 5, change the frequencies to get a mean of 5.1, then 5.2.
- Get a mean of 5 and a mode of 4.
- Get a mean of 6 and a mode of 3.
- How can you work out the median?

The mode can be seen from the chart, but Excel can calculate neither the mode nor the median, because it is expecting to work with raw data, rather than data that has already been organised.

It is probably more realistic to work with raw data and get the spreadsheet to produce the frequency table for you. Excel does this with an array formula, =FREQUENCY(data array, bins array), where the bins are the end of the interval against which the formula counts. The mean, mode and median can be calculated from the raw data (beware of distributions with more than one mode!). You can simulate throwing a dice by generating random numbers

=ROUNDUP(RAND()*6,0)

or the sum on two dice

=ROUNDUP(RAND()*6,0) + ROUNDUP(RAND()*6,0)

or other distributions based on chance – but perhaps that is another objective.

> Change the raw data in the template in Figure 8.9 to obtain a mean of 5.

- Once you have a mean of 5, change the frequencies to get a mean of 5.1, then 5.2.
- Get a mean of 5 and a mode of 4.
- Get a mean of 6 and a mode of 3.
- Get a mean, mode and median of 4.
- Get a mean, mode and median of 5.
- Get a mean of 5, a median of 4 and a mode of 6.

	A	B	C	D	E	F	G	H	I
1		Raw Data					Frequency Table		
2	6	2	1	1	5				
3	1	2	4	6	5		Bin	Frequency	
4	2	3	1	5	2		1	16	16
5	2	4	4	1	4		2	21	42
6	5	5	3	3	5		3	12	36
7	3	4	1	4	2		4	14	56
8	6	2	3	7	1		5	16	80
9	2	5	6	1	6		6	15	90
10	2	7	1	6	6		7	6	42
11	3	5	4	2	5		TOTAL	100	362
12	6	2	2	6	1				
13	3	5	7	4	5		mean =		3.62
14	4	6	6	1	3				
15	4	2	4	5	1				
16	2	2	3	6	1				
17	1	3	4	7	2				
18	4	6	2	1	2				
19	2	1	7	4	5	Mean =	3.62		
20	2	5	6	5	7	Mode =	2		
21	6	3	5	2	3	Median=	4		

Figure 8.9 Raw data to frequency table

Templates such as these become more useful when you deal with grouped data because they allow you to compare the true mean with the estimated mean when you use a mid-interval to calculate the estimate. Figure 8.10 assumes intervals 1–10, 11–20 and so on, giving mid-intervals of 5, 15, etc. The calculations in Figure 8.10 do not show much difference between the true and estimated mean, but you can get wider disparity. Explore!

You can use these templates to explore different distributions and ask questions about how representative the measure of central tendency is. You can also explore measures of skewness, which compare mean and median. The advantage of such

	A	B	C	D	E	F	G	H	I	J	K
1		Raw	Data						Frequency Table		
2	15	11	12	38	45		lb	ub			
3	52	31	61	53	54		Bin	Frequency	mid-int		
4	45	57	33	65	61		1	10	2	5	10
5	21	64	12	32	26		11	20	8	15	120
6	61	33	25	16	58		21	30	5	25	125
7	57	51	35	60	12		31	40	13	35	455
8	51	32	25	39	11		41	50	4	45	180
9	40	67	30	7	37		51	60	12	55	660
10	56	56	2	42	37		61	70	6	65	390
11	17	44	34	51	37		TOTAL		50		1940
12			Mean =	38.22							
13			Mode =	12					mean =		38.8

Figure 8.10 Raw data to grouped data, actual and estimated means

templates is that different distributions can be quickly produced to look at the need for statistics other than the averages, such as range, quartiles and inter-quartile range.

Deciding which measure of central tendency to use is much more dependent on the purpose of that data. For example, if the data in Figure 8.11 (sets of numbers are very easy to create with spreadsheets) show the annual earnings of a workforce, for what purpose would each average be used?

	A	B	C	D	E	F	G	H	I	J	K	L	M
1	14000	14000	14000	14000	14000	18000	19000	23000	23000	23000	65000	Mean =	34404.55
2	14000	14000	14000	14000	14000	18000	19000	23000	23000	23000	67000	Mode =	14000
3	14000	14000	14000	14000	14000	18000	19000	23000	23000	23000	69000	Median =	19000
4	14000	14000	14000	14000	17000	18000	19000	23000	23000	23000	71000		
5	14000	14000	14000	14000	17000	18000	19000	23000	23000	23000	73000		
6	14000	14000	14000	14000	17000	18000	19000	23000	23000	23000	75000	Range =	886000
7	14000	14000	14000	14000	17000	18000	19000	23000	23000	23000	77000		
8	14000	14000	14000	14000	17000	19000	19000	23000	23000	23000	79000	Lower Quartile	14000
9	14000	14000	14000	14000	17000	19000	19000	23000	23000	23000	81000	Upper Quartile	23000
10	14000	14000	14000	14000	17000	19000	19000	23000	23000	23000	83000	Inter-Quartile Range	9000
11	14000	14000	14000	14000	17000	19000	19000	23000	23000	23000	85000		
12	14000	14000	14000	14000	17000	19000	19000	23000	23000	23000	900000		
13	14000	14000	14000	14000	17000	19000	19000	23000	23000	23000	100000		
14	14000	14000	14000	14000	17000	19000	19000	23000	23000	23000	100000		
15	14000	14000	14000	14000	17000	19000	19000	23000	23000	23000	100000		
16	14000	14000	14000	14000	17000	19000	19000	23000	23000	23000	100000		
17	14000	14000	14000	14000	17000	19000	23000	23000	23000	23000	110000		
18	14000	14000	14000	14000	17000	19000	23000	23000	23000	23000	300000		
19	14000	14000	14000	14000	17000	19000	23000	23000	23000	40000	500000		
20	14000	14000	14000	14000	17000	19000	23000	23000	23000	40000	900000		

Figure 8.11 Annual earnings

Of course a simpler interpretation, and one that is more easily tested might be:

> Would you use mean, mode or median to represent this set of data?
>
> 23, 24, 27, 27, 28, 29, 31, 34, 35, 37, 38, 39, 40, 41, 48, 49, 51, 53, 198

This has no connection to statistics, other than interpreting what might be meant by 'represent', but it is easy to mark. In choosing activities for pupils we have to decide why we are teaching statistics and what is going to be assessed.

Summary

In this chapter we have offered a way of working with the examples in the Framework. The examples have been illustrated by activities involving ICT, reinforcing those in Chapter 6, in order to offer you a wider selection to compare.

The pages of examples in the Framework offer a useful source of discussion for planning, mainly because of the way these are presented across the Key Stage. They offer a way of working on teachers' own understanding of progression as well as allowing us to come to terms with an external view of the curriculum and the likely forms of external assessment. Using the examples for department discussion may lead to no changes in your school policy but they do provide useful material for analysis.

Finally

This whole book has been about using the Framework as a professional development agent. New documents provide a basis for discussion within your department. If you use discussion to further your understanding of mathematics and the learning of mathematics, such discussion is valuable. It is also important in the time of imposition because you will be able to justify your decisions from an informed point of view. It is not easy to resist the aspects of imposition that you do not like unless you have rehearsed your arguments with other colleagues. If teachers are to retain their claim to professionalism we need to justify our teaching decisions with intellectual argument.

References

Anghileri, J. (2000) *Teaching Number Sense*. London: Continuum.

Askew, M. *et al.* (1997) *Effective Teachers of Numeracy*. London: King's College London.

Boaler, J. (2000) 'Mathematics from another world: traditional communities and the alienation of learners', *Journal of Mathematical Behavior* **18**(4), 379–97.

Boaler, J. *et al.* (2000) 'Students' experiences of ability grouping – disaffection, polarisation and construction of failure', *British Educational Research Journal* **26**(5), 631–48.

Brown, M. (1993) 'Clashing Epistemologies: The battle for control of the National Curriculum and its assessment'. Inaugural lecture, 20 October 1993, King's College London.

Brown, M. (1999) 'Is more whole class teaching the answer?', *Mathematics Teaching* **169**, 5–7.

Brown, M. *et al.* (1998) 'Is the National Numeracy Strategy research-based?', *British Educational Research Journal* **46**(4), 362–85.

Brown, M. *et al.* (2000) 'Turning our attention from the what to the how: the National Numeracy Strategy', *British Educational Research Journal* **26**(4), 457–71.

Burghes, D. (1999) 'The Kassell Project: an international longitudinal comparative project in secondary mathematics', in B. Jaworski and D. Phillips (eds), *Comparing Standards Internationally*. Oxford: Symposium Books.

Cockcroft, W. H. (1982) *Mathematics Counts: Report of the Committee of Inquiry into the Teaching of Mathematics in Schools*. London: HMSO.

Daniels, H. and Anghileri, J. (1995) *Secondary Mathematics and Special Educational Needs*. London: Cassell.

Denvir, B. and Brown, M. (1986a) 'Understanding number concepts in low attaining 7–9 year olds: I', *Educational Studies in Mathematics* **17**, 15–36.

Denvir, B. and Brown, M. (1986b) 'Understanding number concepts in low attaining 7–9 year olds: II', *Educational Studies in Mathematics* **17**, 143–64.

Department of Education and Science (DES)/Welsh Office (WO) (1991) *Mathematics in the National Curriculum (1991)*. London: HMSO.

Department for Education and Employment (DfEE) (1998) *National Numeracy Project: Framework for Teaching Mathematics, Reception to Year 6*. London: DfEE.

Department for Education and Employment (DfEE) (1999) *The National Curriculum for England: Mathematics*. London: DfEE and QCA.

Department for Education and Employment (DfEE) (2000a) *National Numeracy Project: Framework for Teaching Mathematics: Year 7, Draft 3/00*. London: DfEE.

Department for Education and Employment (DfEE) (2000b) *National Numeracy Project: Framework for Teaching Mathematics: Years 7 to 9, Draft 9/00*. London: DfEE.

Department for Education and Employment (DfEE) (2001) *National Numeracy Project: Framework for Teaching Mathematics: Years 7 to 9*. London: DfEE.

Edwards, A. (2000) 'Researching pedagogy: a sociocultural agenda'. Inaugural lecture, 7 November, University of Birmingham.

Gardiner, A. (2000) 'Acceleration? or Enrichment? Serving the needs of the top 10% in School Mathematics'. Press release for UK Mathematics Foundation, University of Birmingham.

Girling, M. (1977) 'Towards a definition of basic numeracy', *Mathematics Teaching* **81**(4), 1–4.

Hargeave, A. (1994) *Changing Teachers, Changing Times: Teachers' Work and Culture in the Postmodern Age*. London: Cassell.

Hatch, G. (1999) 'It wouldn't be like that here. Some reflections on schools and mathematics teaching in Hungary and the UK', *Mathematics Teaching* **168**, 26–31.

Mahony, P. and Hextall, I. (2000) *Reconstructing Teaching: Standards, Performance and Accountability*. London: Routledge Falmer.

Mason, J. (1991) Inaugural address. Open University, Milton Keynes.

National Curriculum Council (NCC) (1992a) *Using and Applying Mathematics Book A: Notes for Teachers at Key Stages 1–4 NCC*. York: NCC.

National Curriculum Council (NCC) (1992b) *Using and Applying Mathematics Book B: INSET Handbook for Key Stages 1–4 NCC*. York: NCC.

Noss, R. (1997) *New Cultures, New Numeracies*. London: Institute of Education.

Prestage, S. and Perks, P. (2001) *Adapting and Extending Secondary Mathematics Activities: New Tasks for Old*. London: David Fulton

Reynolds, D. (1998) 'Teacher effectiveness: better teachers, better schools (Annual TTA lecture)', *Research Intelligence* **66**, 26–9.

Reynolds, D. and Farrell, S. (1996) *Worlds Apart? A Review of International Surveys of Educational Achievement involving England*, OFSTED Review of Research Series. London: HMSO.

Ruthven, K. (2000) 'The English experience of teaching a "calculator-aware" number curriculum', in J. Anghileri (ed.) *Principles and Practices in Arithmetic Teaching*. Buckingham: Open University Press.

Schmidt, W. H. *et al.* (1996) *Characterizing Pedagogical Flow: An Investigation of Mathematics and Science Teaching in Six Countries*. Dordrecht: Kluwer.

UK Mathematics Foundation (2000) Acceleration? or Enrichment? Serving the needs of the top 10% in School Mathematics. University of Birmingham: UK Mathematics Foundation.

Watson, A. and Mason, J. (1998) *Questions and Prompts for Mathematical Thinking*. Derby: Association of Teachers of Mathematics.